# TAMING THE MONKEY MIND

D0932857

# TAMING THE MONKEY MIND

Venerable
Thubten Chodron

Tynron Press

*First published in 1990 by*
*Tynron Press*
*Unit 3*
*Turnpike Close*
*Lutterworth*
*Leicestershire LE17 4JA*
*United Kingdom*

*ISBN 1-871948-55-X*

*Reprinted 1991, 1992, 1994, 1995*

*Cover by Eric Yeo*
*Typeset by Linographic Services Pte Ltd*
*Printed in Singapore by Vine Graphic Pte Ltd*

**THE DALAI LAMA**

# FOREWORD

I am very happy to know that Ven. Thubten Chodron has prepared her second book: TAMING THE MONKEY MIND, specifically for Asian readers. In the course of living in many parts of Asia, where she had both studied and taught Buddhism, she has acquired a keen appreciation of the misunderstandings that sometimes arise about countries and traditions. Similarly, there is often confusion even in one country about the differences between Buddhist teachings and folk customs.

This book reflects a sincere attempt to help people overcome such misconceptions, showing how to find peace and contentment through a practical application of the teachings of the compassionate Buddha. Ven. Thubten Chodron has chosen a wide variety of situations that we all encounter in daily life and has explained how to deal with them from a Buddhist viewpoint, in words that are easy to understand. In so doing she has made a valuable contribution to peace and human understanding by providing her readers with the opportunity not only to understand a variety of approaches to Buddhist practice, but also to benefit from such practices in their own lives.

July 19, 1990

# INTRODUCTION

A student approached me after a talk at the National University of Singapore. "One of my friends isn't a Buddhist, but she wants to learn about it. Is there an introductory book in simple English, that's easy to understand and explains the essence of Buddha's teachings?"

I knew that question well. In fact, I had searched for such a book, but to no avail. There is a variety of excellent material on Buddhism, but none of it fits the above description.

This started me thinking. Several weeks later, a polytechnic student queried, "Is there a book about friendship, love and marriage, and sex from a Buddhist viewpoint? Something we 20th century young people can relate to?"

Again, I drew a blank. The idea of writing this book was born soon thereafter.

## Overview

*Taming the Monkey Mind* is for anyone interested in the Buddha's teachings. The first section discusses how to have good relationships with others. The second section contains the essence of Buddhist philosophy and psychology, together with practical ways they are put to use in daily life. The third section relates the history and development of Buddhism, and explains the meaning of Buddhist temples, centers, ceremonies and festivals. "Buddhism Today" addresses two potential problems: superstitions and misconceptions about Buddhism, and religious intolerance in our world.

The title of the book, *Taming the Monkey Mind*, was inspired by Lama Yeshe, one of my teachers. He often compared our minds to monkeys: just as monkeys play with an object for a few moments and then leave it in boredom and dissatisfaction to look for another thing to amuse them, so too do we run from thought to thought, emotion to emotion, place to place, trying to find some lasting happiness. Always searching for happiness outside ourselves, we overlook the real cause of happiness and unhappiness: our minds.

Through taming our monkey minds, we can contact our inner beauty and human potential. This book gives an inkling how this is done.

## Language

I've attempted to avoid complicated technical terms as much as possible and to express the Buddha's teachings in clear and simple English. Nevertheless, using some technical terms is unavoidable. Translating these terms into English isn't always easy and sometimes the resulting words — for example, "calm abiding" — sound strange to the ear. However, with time, these words will sound less awkward. Their meaning is given in text and a glossary is provided at the end of the book.

Using he/she or s/he to express the impersonal third-person pronoun is awkward. Thus, "he" and "she" are used alternatively. However, the reference isn't restricted to a person of a particular sex.

## Acknowledgments

My gratitude and respect go first to my teachers, principally His Holiness the Dalai Lama, Serkong Rinpoche and Zopa Rinpoche. Without the kindness and support — both material and moral — of people too numerous to mention, this book couldn't have been written. Still, a few names must be mentioned. The students of the Buddhist societies of Singapore's four tertiary institutes inspired the writing of this book. The members of Dharma Friendship Foundation in Seattle, U.S.A. and Amitabha Buddhist Centre in Singapore, provided the circumstances and encouraged me to write. Heartfelt thanks also go to Steve Wilhelm and Cindy Loth for editing the manuscript and to Lesley Lockwood, Pua Yeow Khoon, Lisa Reinhardt and Yeo Soo Hwa for their valuable suggestions. I also thank Ven. Dhammika, Ven. Jendy, and Ven. Sangye Khadro for checking the chapters on Theravada, Mahayana and Tibetan Buddhism respectively. Credit should be given to Ang Sea Chuan whose painting is shown on the cover of the book. The line drawings are reproduced from *Cho Yang*, a magazine published by by the Tibetan Department for Religious and Cultural Affairs in Dharamsala, India.

# CONTENTS

# I

# OUR RELATIONSHIPS
# WITH OTHERS

*Each of us wonders, "How can I have a happy life? What will help me get along better with other people? How can I solve the problems that arise at work, school and home?"*

*Buddhism addresses these very immediate concerns. For this reason, many people consider the Buddha's teachings to be a practical psychology, a guide to living a happy life. Complex philosophy or rituals aren't necessary to do this: merely a clear perspective on our lives is helpful.*

*This section grew from a request made by young adults in a meditation class I taught. They sought guidelines for having productive and gratifying relationships with others. In the Sigalovada Sutra, the Buddha gave practical advice on the principal realtionships we have in our lives. Part of the following chapters are taken from that sutra, as well as from other sutras and commentaries.*

# PARENT AND CHILD:

*Being close while letting go*

The relationship between parent and child is a unique and precious one, for it's due to the kindness of our parents that we're alive today. This is one of the most changeable of our relationships because it lasts over a long period of time, during which both parents and child as individuals go through many stages in life. Thus, both have to be sensitive to the changes occurring in the other, and to allow and support them.

With the easy availability of birth control, couples can now plan their families. It's wise to wait to have children till when the marriage is stable and there is no financial difficulty in supporting the children. However, if a child comes when it isn't expected, welcome it, for this being now has the opportunity to enjoy a human life.

The Buddha told Sigalo:

Householder, in these five ways the parents discharge their responsibilities towards their children:

1. they restrain them from negative actions,
2. they establish them in virtuous actions,
3. they educate them in the arts and sciences
4. they provide them with suitable wives and husbands
5. they give them their inheritance at the proper time.

Parents should restrain their children from actions that harm either themselves or others. They should encourage their children to share what they have with others and to have a kind attitude towards others. If children are brought up to value ethics and kindness, they'll become happy adults who will get along well with others. If children aren't taught how to be kind and happy people, then even if they have many academic degrees, their lives will be filled with difficulties.

Parents need to be good examples for their children. The old slogan of "do what I say, not what I do," is a limp excuse for parents doing what they advise their children not to. Children copy their parents' actions, and by acting hypocritically, parents are telling their children that hypocrisy and lying are all right. Thus, parents who want to help their children will live ethically and will be kind towards others.

Also, to help their children develop good characters, parents must spend time with them. Although both parents may work to support the home, they should avoid becoming "workaholics." Working overtime to earn more money may seem appealing, but if that extra money has to be used to pay for the children to get counseling because they feel unloved, what use is it? Similarly, if the parents overwork and are very stressed, the money might have to be used to buy tranquilizers, pay for medical bills due to treatment for ulcers and heart attacks. Or they might have to take vacations without the kids so they can relax. Overwork is self-defeating for the parents.

In addition, the children miss out on love and affection from their parents. Even if the parents pay for music and art lessons and sports activities for their children, if the children feel unloved, all their lessons won't enable them to grow up to be happy adults. Western societies are witnessing tremendous increases in crime, drugs, divorce and delinquent children. A lot of this is due to the breakdown of the family structure and the fact that parents don't spend enough quality time with their children. I hope modernizing Asian societies will learn from the mistakes of the West and avoid them. Grasping for money, at the expense of family closeness, brings problems.

Parents should give their children the best education they can, and gear that education towards the child's disposition. If a child doesn't have musical ability, why torture him with forced music lessons? On the other hand, if a child has talent and interest in geology, the parents should encourage that.

In our modern world children are pressured from a young age to learn a lot and strive to be the best. This creates many psychological problems, for children need time to just be children and to have fun. They need to be able to try new activities without being evaluated by tests and without their performance being compared to others. They need to be loved simply for who they are, without feeling they have to be the best.

Clearly, in our present society, parents don't arrange their child's marriage as in ancient India. Also, in those days, the family business — the inheritance — was passed on to the children when they were capable of running it, whereas today that isn't necessarily the case. However, I believe in today's society, the fifth advice could mean that parents provide for the material well-being of the child as best as they can.

Parents should care for the child's physical and material needs in a practical way. Obviously, they can't give more than their income allows. Giving children everything they want doesn't necessarily benefit them, and nagging brats may be produced instead. When children have unfulfilled wishes, parents can help them by explaining that what they want is too expensive or isn't available. It might help them if they understood that even if they had it, it wouldn't make them completely happy and that by making a fuss, they are making themselves more unhappy. Parents should explain to them the benefits of sharing possessions with others.

By helping their children deal with unfulfilled wishes, parents show them how to diminish their attachment, prevent them from taking things for granted, and help them to consider others' needs and wishes. Children often understand more than adults give them credit for. When something is explained calmly, logically and repeatedly, in various circumstances that illustrate the point, children will understand.

Children develop their self-images depending upon what the adults around them say. If children are often told they're naughty or stupid, they'll develop that self-concept and then will become like that. Thus, it's important to praise children and acknowledge what they do.

When correcting children's mistakes, parents should help them understand why that action was harmful. Also, it's important that children learn that although they made a mistake, it doesn't mean that they're bad people. If children start thinking that they — not the action they did — are bad, then that negative self-image will mold who they become.

Sometimes, in order to convey an important point to a child, parents may have to speak forcefully, but their minds should be imbued with compassion, not anger. In that way, they let the child know a certain action is not to be repeated, but they aren't angry and don't reject the child because he or she did it.

Being a parent means walking the fine line between the extremes of over-protecting the children, and neglecting them by not providing sufficient guidance. To counteract excess attachment and possessiveness, parents must remember that their children aren't their possession. Children are unique personalities, who must learn to form their own opinions and make their own decisions.

By being too attached to a child, parents create the circumstance for their own unhappiness, for it's impossible for the child always to be with them. When their children grow up, some parents have difficulty in allowing their children to become more independent, for it means that they can't control their children's actions as closely and must trust the children's ability to make good decisions.

Some parents consistently tell their children what to do and what not to do. There is no discussion involved, for the children are expected simply to do what they're told. There are some situations where this is appropriate — for example, when the child's well-being is endangered and he clearly lacks the ability to decide properly.

However, constantly telling children what to do doesn't help them to develop good judgment. Nor does it allow for them to seek their parents' advice and discuss their problems with their parents. Children feel much closer to their parents if their parents listen and respond to them. When parents explain *why* a certain behavior is harmful or beneficial, it helps children to make wise decisions later. In this way, children learn to think clearly and act beneficially. Having trained their children to do this, parents then will feel more comfortable trusting their children. This helps to avoid the power struggle that so often happens during the teenage years.

Parents can't make their child be what their image of a perfect child is. Each child has his or her own potentials, and these may or may not correspond with what the parents want him or her to be. Parents can't expect their child to live their own unfulfilled dreams. While guiding their child to choose careers, spouses and hobbies, parents must be mindful to have the child's interests, not their own in mind. Wise parents accept their children as they are, while simultaneously guiding them to develop according to their capacities.

The other extreme is neglecting the child, which unfortunately happens too often in busy societies. Sometimes, in order to provide for the children's material well-being, the parents are too busy working to spend time with them or to give the love and guidance that they need. Parents need to allocate their time appropriately. It may be better to work less, but have a more united family.

Parenting is a challenge and can enrich one's Dharma practice. The teachings on impermanence are apparent as the children grow up. The disadvantages of anger and the importance of developing patience become clear when parents lose their temper in frustration at a child they want to help. An inkling of what it would be like to cherish all beings comes when parents think of loving everyone as much as their children. With mindfulness, parents and children can grow at the same time.

## Understanding Our Parents

The topic of children's responsibilities toward their parents is a sensitive one nowadays. In societies where the family structure is breaking down, some children neglect to help their parents. Sometimes, because parents have continuously sought to fulfill the wishes and needs of their children, the children take this kindness for granted and expect their parents to provide everything for them. When children have this attitude, it not only hurts the parents, but also leaves the children feeling disconnected and alone.

Many movements in psychology trace our insecurities and personality characteristics back to events that happened in childhood. Some people misinterpret this and blame their parents for all of their problems. Although it's important to understand the influence our upbringing had on us, we're adopting a victim mentality by considering our parents the source of our problems. Clinging to the past by thinking, "They did this and that, therefore I have problems now," doesn't allow us to grow. We must assume responsibility for our own present insecurities and weaknesses and act to correct them.

Some children do grow up in dysfunctional families with negligent or abusive parents. It's important for these children to seek outside help so that they don't blame themselves for their parents' problems. Nor should children go to the other extreme and blame their parents for their own problems. Blame doesn't help heal emotional wounds. Understanding and forgiveness do.

In general, we're expert in enumerating others' faults, and weak when it comes to remembering their good qualities and kindness. Especially with our parents, it's all too easy to blame them for their shortcomings and the consequent effects these had on us. Our parents may have done things while we were young that affected us negatively, but in their minds, they were doing the best they could given their own internal state of mind and the external circumstances. Thinking like this, we'll understand and forgive our parents, thus relieving the pain that anger and resentment cause.

If we complain that our parents don't understand and accept us for what we are, we also must ask whether we understand and accept our parents for what they are. It's hard to accept that our parents have faults and problems and that we can't make them become the ideal parents we envision. But when we can accept this, we'll be happier.

Children benefit themselves and their parents when they remember the kindness of their parents. Our parents gave us our bodies and took care of us when we were helpless infants. They taught us to speak, gave us an education, and provided for us materially. Without their loving care, we would have starved during infancy or accidentally gotten hurt. As children, we didn't enjoy being disciplined when we misbehaved, but if our parents had not done so, we would have grown up to be rude and inconsiderate adults.

Teenagers often have difficulty getting along with their parents. They view themselves as adults and balk when their parents sometimes treat them as children. To the parents, however, the teenagers are still children and the parents want to protect them. In fact, even when we're 60 years old, our parents still see us as children. I chuckle when my grandmother tells my father (who is 65) to put on a jacket so he doesn't catch cold! If we accept this situation and are patient with our parents, the relationship will be smoother.

Also, it helps if teenagers recognize that their behavior isn't always consistent. Sometimes they want their parents to do many things for them, as if they were children who couldn't take care of themselves. Other times, they want their parents to treat them like self-sufficient adults. No wonder parents are confused! The best way for teenagers to demonstrate to their parents that they're mature is by being kind, helpful and responsible.

Some parents have difficulty adjusting as their children grow up and become more independent. Parents may feel useless and unloved. As a result, some parents get depressed, while others become domineering or interfere with their children's lives. Rather than becoming belligerent at their parents' behavior, children can try to understand and address their parents' feelings. We'll be sensitive to our parents' emotional needs, and we'll reassure them of our love, even though we're more independent.

Sometimes parents see potential dangers that we don't see; sometimes they have a long-range view while we only look at the momentary situation. In these cases, their advice is wise. Although their advice may seem to stifle our desires, often we can understand its value. We don't need to feel that our independence is compromised by following their advice. Rather, we'll see its wisdom and voluntarily will follow it.

If we feel that our parents are being unreasonable, we can try to discuss the situation with them. But first, it's beneficial for us to calm our anger, for if we approach our parents with belligerence, we make it difficult for them to listen to us. Do we listen to people who are rude to us?

Even if our parents are unreasonable, they mean well. They're trying to help us and to guide us as well as they can. Despite their faults, they mostly have good motivations. They may be short-sighted or concerned with things that we consider unimportant, but whatever their limitations are, they mean well. If we remember that, we'll recognize their love for us and won't get angry. We can feel grateful for their concern and then present our viewpoint to them, explaining it in a way that they can understand.

Our parents are conditioned and limited by their own preconceptions and upbringing. They grew up in a different social environment than we did, so naturally they see things differently. From their viewpoint, having grown up the way they did, most of what they think makes sense; just as growing up as we have, our perspective seems right.

If we only think of our parents' weaknesses, then they appear to

8

us as full of faults. Thinking that way makes us ignore the good qualities they have. If we remember their kindness and the care they have shown us, we'll see their good qualities and our hearts will open with love. We won't be stubborn and rude, so our parents will listen more to what we have to say.

The Buddha told Sigalo five ways for children to fulfill their responsibilities to their parents:

1.  They support and protect their parents and supply their wants.
2.  They perform the duties their parents delegate to them.
3.  They maintain the good name of the family.
4.  They conduct themselves in such a way as to deserve the inheritance of parental property.
5.  They give alms in the name of their parents when they are dead, and dedicate the positive potential to them.

It's only fair that children do their share of household chores and work for the benefit of the entire family. And, since parents cared for and supported the children while they were young and helpless, children should happily reciprocate when their parents are sick or aged. If the children can't care for their parents themselves, they'll ensure that someone else does.

Some elderly people are demanding, but if we consider how life appears to them, we'll be more tolerant of the difficulties they have growing old. If we think about how we would feel being them, we'll be more understanding. When we're old, we certainly will want our children to care for us.

To repay the kindness of their parents, children should live according to the good ethical values their parents taught them. The children should conduct themselves well, causing the parents less worry, and also preventing them from being criticized or ashamed. In this way, too, children make themselves worthy of receiving inheritance from their parents.

After the parents' death, children can make offerings and prayers and dedicate the positive potential accumulated by these for their parents' happiness and good rebirth. Of course, if we really want to benefit our family members, it's best while they're alive to encourage them to act constructively and avoid harmful actions. We can act in all the ways mentioned above to have a good relationship with our parents.

# FRIENDSHIP:

*Sharing and caring*

In *The Dhammapada*, the Buddha said:

> Just as the clean kusha grass
> That wraps a rotten fish
> Will also start to rot,
> So too will those devoted to an unwholesome person.

> Just as a leaf folded
> To contain an incense offering
> Also becomes sweet,
> So too will those devoted to the virtuous.

Our friends influence us a lot. Thus our choice of friends affects the kind of people we'll become. We can see how much our companions influence us by looking at our own experiences: think of times when we were unhappy or in trouble and notice how much those situations were due to being with the wrong people. Similarly, think of the happiness we've had and knowledge we've gained being in the company of caring friends.

What qualities make people good friends? Which ones are better to avoid? For the sake of brevity, I've paraphrased the section in the *Sigalovada Sutra* about friendship. Reflecting on each point and thinking of examples from our lives will help us gain clarity about our friendships.

Although the points are expressed in terms of the qualities we want to look for in others, it's equally important for us to check if we have those qualities ourselves. The points are very practical advice on which personality traits to discourage and which to develop in ourselves so that others will be attracted to us and we'll be good friends to others.

There are four kinds of false friends, who are actually foes disguised as friends:

1.    Those who come empty-handed but leave with something. These are people who:
  - visit us with the intention of taking our things,
  - give us a little but expect to receive a lot in return
  - help us only when they're in danger
  - associate with us only out of selfish motives

2.    Those who pay us lip service, and whose friendship is only skin-deep. These are people who:
  - entertain us and waste our time by talking of the past
  - entertain us and waste our time by talking of the future
  - try to gain our favor by offering help when help isn't needed
  - when we ask for help, they give excuses and don't help

3.    Those who flatter us, seeming to care for us when they actually don't. These are people who:
  - encourage us to act negatively
  - discourage us from acting positively
  - praise us in our presence
  - criticize us behind our backs

4.    Those who lead us to our ruin are people who:
  - are our companions in drinking  or taking  drugs
  - roam the streets with us when it's late
  - accompany us to see unwholesome entertainment
  - go gambling with us

Having an open and trusting relationship with people like these is difficult. It's better to keep them at a distance, but without criticizing them. Although we can say some behavior isn't good, we can't say the people who do it are evil, irredeemable people. We can still have compassion for them and wish them well, but we don't seek their company for we know it will lead us in a direction we don't want to go.

Similarly, the Buddha described the qualities of good friends. These are people we can trust and rely on, and by associating with them, we'll be happy and our characters will improve. As well as seeking the company of people with good qualities, it's important to develop these traits within ourselves.

The four kinds of good-hearted friends are:

1.  Those who help us. These people:
    - guard us when we're careless or not paying attention
    - protect our possessions
    - help and console us in times of fear
    - give more than asked for when we request their help

2.  Those who care for us in good times and bad. These people:
    - confide in us
    - keep what we tell them confidential
    - don't forsake us when we're troubled or face calamity
    - would even sacrifice their lives for us

3.  Those who encourage us in a positive direction and cause us to become better people. These people:
    - dissuade us from doing negative actions
    - persuade us to do positive actions
    - cause us to listen to beneficial teachings
    - indicate to us the path to happiness

4.  Those who are compassionate and sympathetic. These people:
    - sympathize with us in times of adversity
    - rejoice at our prosperity and fortune without being jealous
    - dissuade others from speaking ill of us
    - praise those who speak well of us

Although what has been said above is very general, and we may feel we learned it when we were children, it's valuable to reflect on our relationships and actions to see how well we practice this advice now. By taking general principles and applying them to specific situations in our lives, we'll get to know ourselves better and will have a better idea of how we want to grow.

# Love and Attachment

People often wonder how to reconcile the Buddha's teachings on non-attachment with those on love. How can we love others without being attached to them? Non-attachment is a balanced state of mind in which we cease overestimating others' qualities. By having a more accurate view of others, our unrealistic expectations fall away, as does our clinging. This leaves us open to loving others for who they are, instead of for what they do for us. Our hearts can open to care for everyone impartially, wishing everyone to be happy simply because he or she is a living being. The feeling of warmth that was previously reserved for a select few, now can be expanded to a great number of people.

With some people we share many common interests. It's easy to talk to them; we understand each other well and help each other grow. We may spend more time with these people than with others. They can be our friends without our clinging to them with attachment. The focus of such a friendship is mutual growth, not fulfillment of our selfish desires.

Since it's difficult to free ourselves from attachment, initially our friendships will be a combination of attachment and genuine love. But, being aware of the disadvantages of attachment, we'll try to eliminate it so it doesn't cause problems in our relationships. Slowly, the quality of our friendships will improve.

# Helping Our Friends

It's important for us to be sensitive to others' needs and wishes. This involves having respect and appreciation for people as unique individuals. It also entails our not being self-centered and demanding. As soon as we start thinking more of our own benefit than of mutual benefit in a relationship, problems will arise.

Sometimes we have a "take take" mentality. We view everything and everyone in terms of what we can get from them. Neglecting to consider our effect on others, we think only of how others benefit and harm us. This attitude leads us to have problems with others, for no matter what others do or how kind they are, we're never satisfied. We become grouchy and discontent, making ourselves and those around us miserable.

The "take take" mentality shows itself very clearly when we enter a room full of strangers. Do we usually think as we walk in, "How can I benefit the people here? What are their needs? What pain are they experiencing that I can help to remove?" Usually, such an other-centered attitude is far from our minds, and instead we're engrossed wondering, "Who has connections that can help me? Will people ignore me or put me down? Will that good-looking person over there like me?"

It's interesting to pause a moment before going into a room and think, "In this life and in my previous lives, all beings have been kind to me. Now is my chance to return their kindness. No matter what they look like on the surface, these people are just like me — they sometimes feel insecure and want to be appreciated, they like to be acknowledged as worthwhile individuals. I'm going to use this time with them to give whatever I can." Our experience in interviews, at parties and during meetings will be considerably different if we practice thinking like this.

Gradually, we'll develop a "give give" mentality, thinking of what we can do for others. When we have this attitude our own problems don't seem so enormous and we're happy whomever we're with. Others are happy, they like us, and inside our hearts, we're satisfied, for we know that our lives are meaningful.

Part of being sensitive to others involves knowing when to talk and what to say. Let's not waste others' time with our frivolous chatter. This is actually more difficult than it sounds, for we may think something is important and interesting, while others may not. Being aware of others' values and priorities will make us more considerate.

Being considerate and generous doesn't mean we suppress our own self-development in order to do whatever others want. There is a difference between being kind to others out of genuine affection for them and denying our own self-worth to do what others say just to gain their approval. Before we can have a kind heart, we have to have self-respect.

On the other hand, self-respect is different from selfishness. With the former we recognize our worth as human beings, with the latter we cling to our happiness as if it were more important than that of others. A balance point between self-abnegation and selfishness is to recognize the fundamental equality between ourselves and all others: we all seek happiness and to avoid problems. We all have good qualities and weaknesses. We're all worthy of respect simply because we're living beings.

## Peer Pressure

Although we usually think of peer pressure occurring among young people, in fact it influences us regardless of our age or who we associate with. None of us enjoys being insulted or misunderstood and we all want others to think well of us. Although we know that we shouldn't pay attention if certain people ridicule or criticize us, still we are afraid of what they might have to say. As a result, we may join in their activities to receive their friendship and thus avoid their antagonism.

What is at issue is our self-confidence. When we rely on others' praises to feel worthwhile, we go up and down emotionally, depending on what others say. We become extremely vulnerable and are easily influenced because we don't know clearly what we believe, or even if we do know, we lack the confidence to express it.

It's important to contemplate deeply the fact that someone telling us we're good doesn't make us good or that someone criticizing us doesn't make us bad. Praise and blame are only others' impressions and opinions; they're not a part of ourselves. We have to examine our own attitudes and behavior and develop a realistic view of ourselves. In that way, we can assess our own strengths and weaknesses.

If someone accurately points out our weaknesses or mistakes, there's nothing to be alarmed at. It's like someone saying, "There's a nose on your face." It's there for everyone to see, so trying to hide our mistakes is useless. To become offended when someone else notices what is obvious is equally as senseless. Let's just accept that we made a mistake and apologize.

If someone tells us we have horns on our head, we aren't insulted for it's clear the other person is mistaken. Similarly, if we're blamed for something that we didn't do, or if others exaggerate what we did, there's no need to be angry. What they're saying is incorrect.

We all have good qualities, and it's important to acknowledge them. However, there's no reason to be proud of our talents and achievements, for they came about due to the kindness of others. If others didn't teach us and help us, we wouldn't have been successful. In the same way as we can accept our mistakes without resentment, we can receive others' praise without conceit. The Buddha said:

> As a solid rock is not shaken by the wind,
> So too the wise remain unshaken amidst blame and praise.

The ability to be emotionally balanced whether others praise us or blame us, allows us to evaluate and learn from what they say. In this way, we gain a clearer picture of ourselves and thus will be less susceptible to negative peer pressure.

Another factor contributing to our self-confidence is a clear sense of ethical values. When we have this, we won't get confused in potentially harmful situations, nor will we fall prey to the misleading influence of others. If we think deeply about the advantages and disadvantages of certain actions, we'll reach clear conclusions about our ethical values. Even if someone were to criticize or ridicule us for not joining in their unwholesome activities, we would remain unaffected because we'd know that what we're doing is correct. Developing a deep sense of self-confidence and ethical values requires much thought on our part.

## Discussing Problems

Sometimes we need to discuss our problems with friends. How can we do this in a beneficial manner, so that we don't burden them with our difficulties and negative feelings? Sometimes we may need to "let it all out," and a good friend is someone who will listen with an open and compassionate heart.

While it's fine to relate our difficulties to those close to us, it's not very beneficial to dump our emotional confusion onto them and leave it at that. Neither should we tell our problems to our friends merely to gain their sympathy and to have them agree how mean and unfair someone was to us. That only increases our self-pity and doesn't solve our problem!

Once we've acknowledged and accepted that we have a problem, negative feelings or confusion, the next step is to work it out. One way is to seek honest and constructive feedback from our friends. We'll welcome their truthful assessments, even when they tell us we were mistaken or brought on the problem ourselves. Friends, by pointing out when we exaggerate the situation or are inflexible, help us. Instead of telling us we're right even when we're not, our friends will assist us in identifying and solving our problems.

Knowing the value of good friendships, we'll seek the company of those who influence us positively. In addition, we'll try to diminish our faults and increase our good qualities so we can become better friends to others.

# COLLEAGUES AND CLIENTS:

*Working together and resolving differences*

We can develop the lofty goal of becoming Buddhas for the benefit of all beings while we're seated in meditation. But we must also be down to earth and practice love and compassion towards those around us, especially the people we work with. Living ethically, appreciating others' efforts and resolving differences are ways to do this.

## Living Ethically

Ethics form the basis for living together peacefully and prosperously. People who are trustworthy in their jobs not only win the respect of their bosses, colleagues and clients, but also their careers are more successful in the long run. If we charge fair prices, render good service and are honest with clients, they'll continue to do business with us and will refer others to us as well.

On the other hand, neglecting ethics by doing whatever fulfills our selfish momentary purposes brings disharmony and eventually harms our career. In recent years, several prominent people in business and government have been convicted of violating the law and publicly disgraced. Their greed for money and prestige was the source of their dishonesty and eventual downfall.

People hesitate to do business with those who are known to be ruthless. If we lie or are dishonest with our bosses, colleagues or clients, we'll lose their respect and cooperation. Although we may temporarily benefit from selfish ways of conducting business, in the long run we'll be unable to work well with others during the day or to sleep with a clear conscience at night. Abandoning the ten destructive actions will prevent these difficulties.

## Appreciating Others

Helping our colleagues and appreciating their work makes them happy and builds a spirit of teamwork. When others feel their efforts have

19

been recognized, they're more cooperative and work harder. If they are given avenues to air their opinions, they feel more involved and loyal to their company.

But our motivation in praising others shouldn't be just to increase their productivity! Insincerity is quickly uncovered and it spoils working relations. Respecting and appreciating others — including those "inferior" to us in terms of position, education and so forth — is a key element in our development of love and compassion. Therefore, we must remember that a boss can't be successful without the work of her staff, a company can't function without its employees. Our success, therefore, isn't our own: it's due to the kind efforts and cooperation of others. Thus listening to, respecting and praising them is suitable.

Staff and workers too need to recognize the efforts of their bosses. It's easy to complain and criticize and difficult to acknowledge that others do their best, even though they aren't perfect. Although workers should give constructive feedback on unfair company policies, gossiping behind others' backs and fomenting disharmony only create more problems for everyone.

## Resolving Difficulties

As long as we're in cyclic existence, we'll have problems and conflicts with others. They challenge us to be creative in how we communicate and solve our problems. What are ways to do this? First, the Buddha advised:

> Do not look out for others' flaws,
> For what they do or do not do,
> But look out for what one oneself
> Should do and should not do.

Being aware of and responsible for our own attitudes and actions is more effective in having good relations than telling others what they should do. Numerous are the examples of problems arising because we focus more on criticizing others' behavior and gossiping about them, than on what we do. It's easy to point out others' faults, but we don't like to look at our own.

This attitude doesn't bring results we desire. Although we may notice others' weaknesses, we can't correct them. Our own faults, which we have the power to remedy, can't be corrected if we ignore them. Although we can influence others' attitudes and actions, we can never control them, for each person is in charge of his or her own actions, words and thoughts. Thus, demanding that others change is unrealistic. In any relationship, we can only dictate our own behavior, and even that isn't so easy to do!

When differences arise at work, we can approach the situation by first thinking how it appears through the eyes of the other person. This enables us to understand his or her position and feelings, and thereby be understanding rather than angry. We may also discover we accidentally (or even deliberately) did something to disturb the other person. We can then apologize.

Some people resist apologizing for fear of losing face. However, by refusing to admit their mistakes, they increase the tension and bad feelings. In actual fact, people who are able to apologize are courageous. They speak not from a position of weakness, but one of strength because they have the self-confidence and integrity to admit and remedy their mistakes. Only a cowardly person hides his errors and stubbornly refuses to admit them.

However, if upon investigation, it seems we haven't erred, then we should talk directly with the other person to resolve the misunderstanding or disagreement. This should be done without anger, after having calmed our minds by applying the techniques the Buddha taught for subduing anger.

Then we can express the problem to our colleague, for example, without accusing or blaming him, for that only worsens the situation by putting him on the defensive. Rather, we can say, "When you act like this, I feel upset because..." and explain why we feel this way. In this way, we're owning up to our feelings, rather than blaming them on the other person. Also, we're explaining to our colleague the impact his actions have on us and why we feel the way we do. We can then add, "I'm not happy feeling like that. Please explain why you do this, so I can understand."

21

In such a way, we give the other person space to explain his viewpoint. When he responds, we should try to listen and understand what he says, without interrupting. Sometimes this requires great patience on our part, for the temptation to interrupt and explain why he's wrong is great, but in the end, listening with an open mind allows dialogue to follow.

In situations of conflict, it's helpful to think of ourselves and the other person being side by side, approaching the problem together. Rather than envision the two parties as opponents in a battle which will have a winner and a loser, we can see it as a mutual problem needing mutual cooperation to resolve. In that way, we will collaborate to find a solution beneficial to both of us.

Sometimes we may be jealous of our colleagues. This painful emotion can be resolved by viewing our colleagues' success from a different perspective. If they have qualities, talents or opportunities that we don't, we can rejoice at their happiness. We aren't the only one who seeks happiness, others also do. Besides, we often say, "Wouldn't it be wonderful if everyone were happy!" Now we must make our feeling consistent with our words. Our colleague is successful and we didn't have to do anything to make her happy! This is cause for rejoicing, not for painful jealousy. By rejoicing at another's fortune, both of us are happy!

In this way, constructively relating to people at work becomes our Dharma practice. It challenges us to integrate the Buddha's teachings with our minds, so that the teachings aren't mere intellectual knowledge but become part of our personality. This not only enables us to progress along the path, but also makes our present relationships more harmonious.

# MARRIAGE:

*Helping each other grow*

All that has been said above regarding selecting friends and the manner in which friends treat each other applies equally to the relationship between boyfriend and girlfriend or husband and wife. This is because friendship and common interests are essential in order to form a firm foundation for a man-woman relationship. Rather than having a relationship based on sexual attraction or excess emotional dependency, a couple will have a more lasting and satisfying relationship if they're friends who trust, encourage and are patient with each other.

It must be added that not all people wish to have a partner. This is an individual choice, depending on each person's character and on other factors. If some people choose to remain single, this could be the best way for them to be happy and productive. Marriage is not for everyone.

Pop music and films present us with an idealistic view of man-woman relationships. If we take this as our example, we run into problems because we're searching for Mr. or Ms. Perfect. Attachment makes us project qualities onto another person or exaggerate the good qualities he or she has, and we're caught in a whirlwind of excitement and romance.

Eventually the bubble pops. This happens not because we or the other person did something wrong, but because we had unrealistic expectations and didn't give the other person the space to be him or herself. Or, we may have had dreams of a perfect relationship free from disagreement. These false expectations created by attachment only lead us to disappointment.

It's much better to be aware that the other person has both good qualities and weaknesses, and that the relationship will have ups and downs. Sometimes two people will be very close and at other times they won't be as close. This is natural, and we should expect it.

It's impossible for another person to fulfill us completely. Why? Because he or she has limitations, and our mind isn't constant. What we want and expect from another is subject to change.

Likewise it's impossible for another to solve all of our problems and insecurities. Only we can solve our problems by practicing the appropriate antidotes to free ourselves from anger, attachment, close-mindedness, jealousy and pride. Understanding this, we'll have patience, mutual respect and ability to forgive, enabling the relationship to grow and continue.

When two people enter into a man-woman relationship seeking self-satisfaction, each one considers his or her personal wishes and needs more important than the other's. This is the basis of all quarrels. This selfish attitude leads to a dead-end, for each party refuses to relinquish his or her desires. Our job is to subdue our own self-cherishing attitude, not to nag the other person to get rid of his or hers.

Marriage is an opportunity to practice cherishing others more than ourselves. A relationship will be stable and enduring if both people think the main purpose of being together is to help each other and to help others. If one person is upset by a disturbing attitude, the other will encourage him or her to look at the situation from a different viewpoint. Or, if both people are in the habit of having quiet time alone to think, and one becomes distracted and neglects his or her quiet time, the other will gently encourage him or her to re-focus on personal and spiritual development. Such mutual support and encouragement strengthens their relationship.

Mutual respect is crucial in a marriage, and this is shown through how we speak and act towards the other. Slanderous or reproachful language doesn't lead to harmony. Neither does any type of physical violence. When we're angry, we make everyone miserable if we vent it on those near us. Being sarcastic, condescending, or teasing our partner about a sensitive issue doesn't bring happiness to either of us.

If we develop respect for both ourselves and our partner, we'll think before we speak because we'll care about the effect our words have on the other. We'll show our respect by caring for mutual possessions, as well as our partner's personal belongings. If he or she has interests or engages in activities that we don't share in, we won't mind, for we'll recognize that the other person isn't our personal property: he or she is a unique individual who wants to develop many sides of his or her personality.

Respect is equally necessary when relating to our partner's family. Whether or not we like our in-laws, it's important to speak and act

24

towards them with consideration. That doesn't mean we let them run our lives, for they may have different priorities or a different life style from ours. However, we can still listen to others' advice and thank them for it, although we may or may not follow it. Being belligerent to our in-laws doesn't create harmony, while respecting them as human beings does. Being jealous of our partner's affection for his or her family also creates tension. It's much better if we respect their care for each other.

Trust is important and is built up by both people being caring and responsible in carrying out their commitments. With the change in gender-identified roles of men and women in our society, each couple needs to divide the duties of running a household and raising a family in a fair way, agreeable to both people. Each person then fulfills his or her responsibilities, thus increasing the trust between them.

Trust is also built up by being truthful to the other person. Thus, it's good to avoid doing things that we have to lie about. If we do make a mistake, let's apologize. On the other hand, if our partner apologizes to us, we should forgive him or her, and try to let go of any hurt feelings or wish for revenge.

Fidelity is another way to maintain and increase trust in a marriage. If we're dissatisfied and desire another sexual partner, we should examine where this attitude comes from. Does it point to a problem in the relationship that we need to discuss and solve with our partner? Or are we merely itchy, bored and fantasizing? In this case, we can remind ourselves that acting on this dissatisfaction will only cause confusion and pain for ourselves, our partner, our children and the third person. It's important to remember the effects our actions have on others. By caring more about others' feelings and less about our own whims, we won't have extramarital sexual relationships.

Trust must also be cultivated in managing the family's money. Each couple should discuss and decide how to handle their money. Whatever is decided upon, we must take care to follow the agreement. Squandering the family's money for our own pleasure, gambling, or spending more than the budget can support, impedes mutual trust, as well as causes financial problems. For that reason, it's wise to consult the other person before making a major purchase, and if that person has strong reservations, to wait. If we respect our partner and cherish him or her, we'll not use money as a tool of power over the other, nor for our own selfish pleasure.

Whether we marry or not is our own personal decision. In Buddhism, marriage isn't a holy matter, and there's no obligation to marry in order to perform a religious duty. Neither is it obligatory for a married couple to have children. A couple may want to have more time for Dharma practice or social welfare projects, in which case they may agree not to have children. Other couples may feel that having a family is important. It's their personal decision whether or not to have children and how many to have.

When parents share a common view of how to raise the children, children don't get confused about what they may and may not do. Children need consistent guidance from both parents. If a parent is inconsistent in his or her actions towards the children, or if the parents teach or do things that contradict each other, the children become very confused. This also could lead to quarrels between the parents. Frequent discussion and good communication between parents will prevent or solve this difficulty.

It may happen that although a husband and wife try to resolve their conflicts, they are unsuccessful and after a while, feel that it's difficult to continue living together. Just as marriage is a secular matter in Buddhism, so are separation and divorce. There is no religious stigma against it. If either person wishes to remarry, he or she may.

However, Buddhism encourages cooperation and harmony among people, as well as patience and forgiveness when differences occur or detrimental actions are done. Married people should do their best to be aware of and be considerate of their spouse's feelings. Running from one person to another or from one situation to another in search of more and better happiness, is a fruitless quest, which only breeds more dissatisfaction. Thus, whenever possible, it's better for a couple to work out their marital difficulties, especially for the sake of the children.

Regarding this, His Holiness the Dalai Lama counseled in *Kindness, Clarity and Insight*:

It is not sufficient that a couple think of only their own love affairs and their own pleasure. You have a moral responsibility to think of your children. If the parents divorce, the child is going to suffer, not just temporarily, but for his or her whole life. The model for a person is one's own parents. If the parents are always fighting and finally divorce, I think that unconsciously, deep down, the child is badly influenced, imprinted. This is a tragedy. Thus, my advice is that for real marriage, there is no hurry: proceed very cautiously, and marry only after good understanding; then you will have a happy marriage. Happiness in the home will lead to happiness in the world.

Thus, if people approach marriage with a realistic attitude, commitment, humility, patience, respect and sincere care for the other person, they will learn and grow through the years. To possess these qualities, we need to reflect on our actions, modify any harmful thoughts or deeds, and cultivate our good qualities.

# SEXUAL RELATIONSHIPS:

*Enjoying them wisely*

The essence of the Buddha's teaching may be expressed: "Help others as much as possible. If you are unable to help others, then at least do not harm them." Actions which harm others not only disturb their well-being, but also create negative karma, which causes us to experience unhappiness in the future. Actions which benefit others increase their happiness and cause us to have happiness in the future.

To understand the Buddhist views of sexual ethics and behavior, we first must understand certain principles central to Buddhist thought. These include the functioning of cause and effect and the disadvantages of disturbing attitudes such as attachment. Both of these subjects will be covered in future chapters. The following discussion is based on the Tibetan sage Lama Tzong Khapa's explanation of unwise sexual behavior in his book, *The Great Exposition of the Gradual Path.*

With this basic Buddhist perspective as the background, we can look at sexual ethics and behavior. When the Buddha spoke of unwise sexual behavior, the principal action he advised against was adultery. Adultery occurs when we're involved in a relationship and we have sex with another person, or when we're single and have sex with someone who is involved in another relationship.

This is harmful because it disrupts the lives of many people: ourselves, our partner, and the children in either family. Hurt feelings, jealousy, mistrust and other problems arise in the lives of ourselves and others. Adultery can cause us to lie, slander, speak harshly to or even take the life of another.

Although many of us grew up in the era of free love and we intellectually propounded many ideals about free sexual relationships, it may be wise to see if our rhetoric works. How do we really feel inside when our partner has a relationship with someone else? Do we honestly feel good about ourselves when we're unfaithful to our partner?

The disadvantages of adultery are evident not only in this life, but also in future lives. By doing a harmful action, we create the potential to have an unfortunate rebirth. We'll have relationships fraught with infidelity, and we'll be inclined to commit adultery again in future lives. In addition, the environment where we take birth will be muddy and unpleasant.

It's interesting to think of these results in terms of what we see happening to ourselves and others now, for what we're experiencing in the present are results of our past actions. For example, a person may be married to someone who is continually having affairs. Their marriage isn't harmonious and is plagued with insecurity and jealousy. Even when that person divorces and remarries, the new partner also isn't faithful and lies to cover it up. It seems that no matter whom this person is involved with, the relationship lacks trust and honesty.

From a karmic viewpoint, we'd say that the person is experiencing the result of adultery committed in previous lives. If he or she hadn't created the cause previously, the result wouldn't have happened. Even if the person had committed adultery in previous lives but had purified the karmic impression, the result wouldn't have occurred. Understanding this gives us more respect for the functioning of cause and effect and helps us decide how we want to act. Because we don't want to experience unpleasant results, we'll do our best to avoid creating the causes, or to purify them if we have.

Interestingly, there is no injunction in the Buddha's teachings against polyandry or polygamy. It seems that sexual misconduct occurs when we step outside the relationships we have committed ourselves to publicly.

While adultery is the chief action to be avoided in the explanation of unwise sexual behavior, there are several auxiliary guidelines regarding unsuitable time, person, manner, or place of having sexual relations.

An unsuitable time is, for example, while the woman is menstruating. A woman is *not* considered "contaminated" during her period, nor is she to refrain from religious activities during that time. I believe intercourse is discouraged during menstruation in consideration for her comfort.

Also, when a woman is pregnant, intercourse can cause discomfort to the child in her womb. The mind of another being enters the fetus at the time of conception. That being experiences pain and pleasure. When a couple is involved in intercourse, the movement and pressure may make the baby uncomfortable.

Another case of improper time is when either partner has engaged in the Buddhist practice of taking the eight one-day precepts. One of the precepts is to avoid sexual contact during that 24 hour period. If either partner has taken those precepts, it would be unwise to transgress them by having sexual contact that day.

It's recommended not to have intercourse during the daytime. Although I haven't heard the exact reason for this, my supposition is that in ancient India, many people lived together in one room. If a couple were to be engaged in sex during the day, another family member could accidentally enter the room, embarrassing everyone. Another possible explanation is that the daylight hours are for working.

Also, having intercourse many times consecutively is discouraged because it encourages excessive desire. We may wonder, "If desire is one of the principal causes for beings to remain in cyclic existence — taking one body after another with constantly recurring problems found in each life — then why does Buddhism only discourage excessive desire and not desire in general?"

In fact, Buddhism does discourage all uncontrolled desire which causes rebirth in cyclic existence. Monks and nuns take the vow of celibacy with the determination to be free of cyclic existence. They then seek to diminish their desire not only by keeping vows, but also by doing appropriate meditations to reduce or transform desire and its energy. This enables them to attain spiritual realizations more quickly.

However, not everyone practices the Buddha's teachings that intensely. We practice the Dharma according to our own ability, and in the case of lay people, this means diminishing excessive desire.

Although at very high levels on the tantric path, a lay bodhisattva practitioner may engage in what appears to be sexual relations, in fact it's very different from ordinary sex. Such practitioners have received advanced teachings from their spiritual masters on how to use sexual energy in meditation to make manifest a subtle consciousness that realizes the emptiness of inherent existence.

People shouldn't fool themselves by thinking they're engaged in a high tantric practice when in fact they're having ordinary sex. Nor it is wise to belittle the value of celibacy vows. People need only ask themselves, "Could I be a monk or a nun?" to discover that they're attached to having sexual relations and don't wish to give them up.

Another instance of an unsuitable time is when either partner is ill, and having sexual relations would aggravate or spread the sickness. This is especially pertinent in the case of sexually transmitted diseases. The essence of the Buddha's teachings is not to harm others and to help them as much as possible. Therefore, we shouldn't have sexual relations if we suspect or know that we have any disease, parasites, etc. that could be transmitted to the other person.

Similarly, out of self-respect, we avoid sexual relations with someone whom we suspect or know has a disease that could be transmitted to us. It's important to keep our bodies healthy in order to practice the Buddha's teachings and to be of benefit to others.

An unsuitable person with whom to engage in sexual intercourse would be a very close blood relative, a child, an animal, one with celibacy vows, or someone who doesn't consent to the act. Incest is advised against because of possible genetic deformities or diseases that could be passed to the child. In addition, incest causes emotional confusion in the minds of many family members. Child molesting harms the child emotionally and mentally, as does having sex with an unconsenting person.

The Buddha didn't speak specifically about premartial sex. We can infer that if both parties are consenting adults, then they're responsible for their own actions, so long as what they do doesn't harm others. However, if one of the people involved is young and under the control of his or her parents, and if having intercourse with that person would upset the parents and the family, then it's wise not to do it, out of consideration for the feelings of others.

There is a wide range of opinions regarding homosexuality in various Buddhist groups. In general, Buddhists are very tolerant towards all people. People aren't to be judged or discriminated against if they are gay.

If masturbation can be avoided, that's better. But, while masturbation isn't encouraged, it's important that a person is not made to feel guilty because of doing it. We need to think deeply and find a way to explain to young people, who have strong physical urges for sex, how to handle this energy. Making them feel bad about themselves for having physical desire doesn't benefit them.

Buddhism has a similiar attitude about doing anything: it's useless to feel guilty or make another person feel guilty for doing something, as guilt only immobilizes us emotionally. Rather, through the four opponent powers, we can purify the negative imprint on our mindstreams. These four are: regretting the action, taking refuge and generating an altruistic attitude toward all beings, doing a remedial action and determining not to do the harmful act in the future. Employing this method for purification is certainly more productive than feeling guilty and being psychologically burdened for our entire life.

Unsuitable manner of sexual practice include any brutal or violent practices, as well as unsuitable orifices, such as the mouth and anus. The advice regarding those orifices for sexual contact is given to prevent health problems and to avoid excessive attachment and desire from arising.

An unwise place for sexual intercouse is in front of a shrine, an image of the Buddha, our spiritual master, parents, a crowd, or in an unhealthy place such as wet or rocky ground. Buddhist families generally don't have a shrine in their bedrooms for this reason. If we live in a single room or have a picture or statue of the Buddha near our bed, then we can put up a screen or put a cloth over the shrine before having sexual relations.

It's important that the society care for people who have AIDS and other such illnesses. To ostracize them is to forget human kindness; to neglect them is to ignore our responsibility for others' welfare. In addition, we should encourage the dissemination of correct information about AIDS and the use of preventive measures.

## Birth Control

A couple can decide whether or not to use birth control to prevent pregnancy. There is no injunction against it. However, once conception has occurred, another being's consciousness has entered the fertilized egg. Thus, it's better to use birth control methods other than the "morning after pill" and the IUD.

Artificial insemination, either by the husband or an anonymous donor, doesn't seem to create harmful effects for self or others. Of course, everyone involved should be in agreement and later abide by that agreement in order to avoid problems.

The Buddhist approach to sexual ethics and behavior is based on the principle of not harming others and benefiting them as much as possible. It also takes into account the functioning of cause and effect over many rebirths. Ethical values aren't commandments given by the Buddha. They're guidelines which the Buddha described so we could create the causes for happiness and avoid the causes for difficulties. Each person is responsible for trying to understand these guidelines as well as possible, and to act according to his or her understanding.

When educating young people about sex, it's best for them to understand why certain guidelines are given. They get distorted ideas if sex education is presented as a detailed series of "don'ts."

Parents and educators need to help young peole understand and accept the physical urges of their bodies and the fantasies of their minds, without making them feel guilty. At the same time, they must be told constructive ways to deal with their physical and mental desires. We need to give a lot of thought to this.

# SPIRITUAL MENTOR:

*Realistically relating to a spiritual guide*

Some people wonder if it's necessary to have a spiritual master. Can we teach ourselves and discover the path alone? Can't we learn from books? To learn worldly skills, for example reading, carpentry, surgery or even driving a car, we need to be taught. It's difficult to learn on our own, and it could even be dangerous. Imagine trying to teach ourselves to pilot a plane! If we depend upon teachers to learn ordinary skills, then certainly we'll need the guidance of qualified teachers for spiritual matters, which are more profound and influence not only this life, but many future lives as well.

A living teacher can do what a book can't: answer our questions, act as an example of how to practice the teachings in daily life, encourage and inspire us on the path, and correct our behavior. Books can enrich and expand what we learn from our teachers, but they can't replace the spiritual relationship we form with a few wise people on the path.

The Sanskrit term for teacher, spiritual master and spiritual mentor — all of which are synonymous — is "guru." This refers to someone who is "weighty in good qualities." The Tibetan term "lama" means unsurpassable.

There isn't an examination to pass to become a teacher. Rather, when others request someone for teaching and guidance, that person becomes their mentor. Some people are commonly referred to as "lama" or "master." This is because they have many students. However, whether they become *your* teacher is up to you. Similarly, other people may not be generally known as "lama" or "teacher," but if we choose them as our teachers, then they become our spiritual mentors.

When we're first learning about Buddhism, we may not have a specific spiritual master. That's fine. We can learn from a variety of teachers and practice accordingly. People who have only a general interest in Buddhism probably won't select a master. However, after a while, people who are serious in their practice will feel the need to establish a teacher-student relationship with spiritual masters so they can receive closer guidance.

# Choosing Our Spiritual Mentors

Because our spiritual mentors will have a great influence on us, it's important to choose them carefully. We don't marry just any person. We first look at the other's qualities and weaknesses, see if our dispositions are similar, and check if we feel we can care for that person through thick and thin. Similarly, it's advisable to examine a person before taking him or her as our spiritual mentor.

Nowadays, we're faced with a spiritual supermarket: there are many teachers to choose from. Anyone can teach one philosophy or another, put on a good show and win over followers. But if we're sincere seekers, we won't be interested in theatrics and showmanship; we'll look for substance.

It may take time to find and identify our masters. To start, we can attend talks and learn from people without accepting them as our masters. This enables us to examine both their character and our ability to relate to them well. We can take our time in deciding whether to take someone as our master: the great Indian sage Atisha examined the renowned master Serlingpa for 12 years before taking him as his spiritual mentor.

It's not advantageous to select people as our spiritual mentors simply because they have many titles, sit on high seats or wear impressive robes or hats. We shouldn't look for pomp but for good qualities. Also, we shouldn't select someone just because he or she is our friend's teacher. We must choose ourselves, according to the teacher's qualities and our experience with him or her.

In the *Mahayanasutralamkara*, Maitreya outlined ten qualities of excellent masters. We should look for people who have:

1.   Pure ethics. Our teachers set an example for us. Because we need to modify our unruly actions of body, speech and mind, it's wise for us to choose teachers who have done so. They will instruct us how to improve ourselves and will be good examples for us to follow.

2.   Experience in meditative concentration.

3.   Deep understanding of the teachings on wisdom. These first

three qualities show that someone is well trained in the Three Higher Trainings which lead to liberation — ethics, concentration and wisdom.

4.    More knowledge and deeper realization of the subject to be taught than we do.

5.    Enthusiastic perseverance to teach and guide their students. If we choose a person who doesn't enjoy teaching or is reluctant to guide others, we won't be able to learn very much.

6.    Extensive learning from competent teachers. We want to learn from those who know the scriptures well and will teach according to them. People who make up their own teachings or misunderstand the Buddha's teachings can't show us the path to enlightenment.

7.    Correct conceptual understanding or direct meditative insight into emptiness.

8.    Skill to articulate the Dharma clearly so we'll understand it correctly.

9.    Motivation of loving-kindness and compassion. This is a very important point. We can't trust someone who teaches in order to receive offerings and respect. There is danger that we'll be led astray by such a person, thereby wasting our lives and potentially engaging in negative activities. Therefore, it's extremely important to select as our masters people who have a pure and genuine wish to benefit their students and lead them on the path to enlightenment.

10.   Patience and willingness to teach people of all levels of intelligence. We aren't perfect and will make mistakes due to our disturbing attitudes of anger and attachment. We need teachers who won't abandon us, but instead will be patient and forgive us. In addition, we want teachers who won't be discouraged when we don't understand what they teach.

It may be difficult to find teachers with all of these qualities. In that case, the most important attributes they should have are:

1. They have more good qualities than faults,
2. They regard creating the ethical causes for happiness in future lives more important than enjoying the pleasures of this life,
3. They cherish others more than themselves.

It's interesting that clairvoyance isn't mentioned as one of the qualities to look for in a master. There is a reason for this. Some people have clairvoyant powers but don't have knowledge of the path to enlightenment. Their clairvoyant powers are due to their previous karma, not to their Dharma practice, and thus they may not use their powers for altruistic purposes. Therefore, in seeking teachers to lead us on the path to enlightenment, we should look for the qualities that Maitreya mentioned.

To learn what qualities teachers have, we should examine their behavior, their understanding of Dharma and how they treat their students. It's not wise to ask Dharma teachers, "Are you enlightened?" for even if they were, they wouldn't tell us. The Buddha forbade his disciples to declare publicly what attainments they have. He wanted his followers to be humble, sincere and unpretentious. Worldly people love to brag about their accomplishments. Spiritual people shouldn't be like this: their goal is to subdue the ego, not to enhance it.

When we have decided  that we would like someone to be our master, we can ask him or her personally to accept us as students. However, this isn't necessary; some masters are very busy with many students, so it's difficult to see them privately. In this case, we can make a strong mental decision  that someone is our spiritual master. After that, when we again hear teachings from that person, he or she becomes our teacher. Also, if we take refuge, precepts or empowerment (initiation) from someone, he or she automatically becomes our spiritual mentor.

We may have several spiritual masters, yet one remains the most important to us and is the one to whom we refer all serious matters.

This master is called our "root spiritual master." This person is the one either who first made the Dharma touch our hearts and firmly set us on the path or with whom we feel the closest connection.

## Following Our Mentors' Instructions, but Not Blindly

Having chosen a person as our spiritual mentor, we should then follow that person's Dharma instructions to the best of our ability. In that way, we'll progress on the path.

Some people are fickle in their relationships with their masters, and run from one master to another until they find one who tells them what they want to hear. Such students make little progress because of their own lack of commitment and respect.

We should care for our teachers' needs, and offer both our service and the requisites they need to live. When we appreciate the kindness of our teachers in showing us the path to happiness, then we'll happily want to help them. As our teachers are working for the benefit of others and for the spread of the Dharma, our offerings will be put to good use.

Our Dharma practice is the best offering to make to our teachers. If we have material possessions, talents and time, we can offer those. However, we shouldn't neglect our practice, for that is what our teacher cares about most. When we follow the Dharma instructions we've received and keep whatever precepts we've taken, that pleases our teacher more than anything else.

When we notice what appear to be faults in our masters, it's counter-productive to criticize them angrily. Often we see faults in others simply because we're projecting onto their actions the motivation we would have if we acted like that. However, that may not be our teachers' motivation; they may do things for completely different reasons, different from what we've supposed. In fact, our master may behave in a certain way to show us what we look like when we act like that.

It's easy for us to find faults in anyone and everyone, but doing so isn't advantageous if we're spiritual practitioners striving to develop tolerance and love. If we angrily criticize and reject our masters, we close the door to benefiting from all of their good qualities. That is a great loss.

However, if our master does something that seems contrary to the Buddha's teachings, we can ask him or her to explain that action. Or, we can simply keep our distance, and not take that behavior as an example of how we should act.

We relate to spiritual teachers to increase our wisdom and self-responsibility. Blindly following someone because "that person is my master, therefore whatever he does is divine" isn't acting intelligently. If our spiritual master asks us to do something that we're not able to do or that we feel isn't right, we should respectfully tell him or her that we're unable to do that.

## Being Honest

Our spiritual mentors are our best friends, and we should try to speak and act honestly with them. Some students are two-faced: they act well in the presence of their teachers, but at other times they gossip, lose their temper and mistreat others. This is counter-productive.

Nor should we try to win our teachers' favor by pretentious sweet talk. Who are we fooling? Our masters care about the state of our minds, not about how we appear superficially.

It's hypocritical to be kind to our teachers and rude to others. Our teachers want all beings to be happy, and thus we contradict our teachers' advice when we're belligerent and mean to others. If we hold our teachers in high esteem and other beings in contempt, we haven't understood the true meaning of the Dharma. To progress on the path, we need to treat both our teachers and other people with respect.

Let's think deeply about the meaning of respect. Some people confuse respect with fear, and then are painfully shy and afraid of doing something wrong near a religious practitioner. There's no need to be emotionally immobilized like this. Interestingly, it may be our selfish mind which is afraid to look bad or foolish in front of someone else.

On the other hand, we shouldn't treat our masters like casual friends. A balance is required: we should endeavor to have a good motivation and act well both when we're with mentors and when we aren't. But at the same time, we shouldn't be afraid to admit our bad qualities to them. We can be honest with our teachers and seek their advice on how to improve.

## Cherishing Our Teachers vs. Being Attached to Them

Some people confuse commitment to their teachers with attachment to them. This can be very painful, for if our teachers don't give us as much attention as we want, we then feel rejected. Attachment causes us to cling to our masters for emotional security, praise and attention. But as we develop true appreciation of our teachers, we'll recognize their qualities and will be grateful for their kindness.

Attachment is self-oriented, while cherishing our teachers is based on sincere spiritual aspirations. Of course, we may miss our teachers when we're separated from them for a long time, but we must ask ourselves if we're missing them because we want Dharma teachings and guidance or because we want to feel loved.

The purpose of having a Dharma teacher isn't to please our egos, but to destroy our ignorance and selfishness by practicing the teachings. When our teachers point out our faults we should be happy they care for us enough to do this. They trust we'll welcome their advice rather than be offended. One time I saw a master tell a student his mistakes at a large gathering. I thought, "That must be a close disciple, for the master knows that person wants to eliminate his egotistical pride and won't mind being publicly reprimanded." In fact, when I got to know the disciple, I discovered he was indeed a good practitioner.

Our relationships with our teachers will grow and develop over time. They can be very rewarding relationships, for by depending on wise and compassionate spiritual guides, we'll enhance our good qualities and eliminate our unwholesome ones. The closeness we feel with our spiritual mentors, who are genuinely concerned with our welfare and progress, is unlike the relationships we have with others. Our teachers will never stop helping us, no matter what we do. While this isn't a license for us to act recklessly, we needn't feel insecure that our teachers will cut off the relationship when we make mistakes. Our spiritual mentors are forgiving and compassionate, and therefore we can trust them.

As our understanding of the path to enlightenment deepens, so will our feeling of closeness with our teachers. This occurs because our minds become more similar to theirs. As our determination to be free increases and our altruistic motivation develops, we'll feel naturally close with our teachers, for we'll have the same interests and goals. Developing the wisdom realizing emptiness diminishes the feeling of separation that is caused by grasping at inherent existence. Eventually, when we become Buddhas, our realizations will be the same as our teachers'.

# II

## AN OUTLOOK ON THE WORLD AND A WAY OF LIFE

*We may wonder, "How did I get here? Why was I born? Who am I and why do certain things happen to me and not to others? How does my mind influence my experience?"*

*To find the answers, we start to look beyond this present life to our situation in general, and we seek solutions to unsatisfactory conditions on a wider scale. What is our potential as human beings? Who can guide us to actualize it and what direction do we take to do so? As our view broadens and deepens, so does our ability to make our lives meaningful through developing compassion and wisdom.*

# MIND IS THE CREATOR OF
# OUR EXPERIENCE

Mind is the forerunner of all actions,
All deeds are led by mind, created by mind.
If one speaks or acts with a corrupt mind,
Suffering follows, as wheels follow the hoof of a draught-ox.

Mind is the forerunner of all actions,
All deeds are led by mind, created by mind.
If one speaks or acts with a serene mind,
Happiness follows, as surely as one's shadow.

*The Dhammapada*

According to Buddhism, our minds are the creators or sources of our experience. This has profound significance: because we each have a mind that we have some degree of control over, we are ultimately responsible for our own experiences. It's unrealistic to blame others for our problems if our own energy is the source of these problems. Similarly, to experience happiness, we needn't placate an external being, but must create the cause for happiness within ourselves by developing positive states of mind.

The Buddhist meaning of "mind" refers to the entire spectrum of perceptions, emotions and cognitions that we have. It also includes what in English we call "heart" (as in "he has a good heart"). The mind isn't just the intellect, nor is it the physical organ of the brain. Formless, the mind isn't made of atoms, so it can't be seen or measured with scientific instruments.

The mind is what experiences pleasure and pain, what thinks, sees, hears, smells, tastes' and touches. The mind is clarity and awareness, for it reflects objects of perception and becomes involved with them. Although the term "our mind" may be used, it doesn't refer to a universally shared mind, but to each of our individual minds. "Mindstream" refers to the continuity of mind from moment to moment.

There are two principal ways our minds create our experiences. First, the mind motivates our actions, or karma. The imprints of our actions are stored on our mindstreams. When these karmic imprints mature, they influence the situations we encounter. Second, our minds interpret and discriminate whatever we contact, thus filtering our perceptions. By doing this, our minds determine how we experience the events in our lives. Let's examine these two points in more depth.

## Mind as the Creator of Karma

In *The Rice Seedling Sutra*, the Buddha described how our lives are the results of our actions, and how these actions originated from our minds. Ignorance is the source. Ignorance produces other disturbing attitudes, such as anger and attachment. Motivated by disturbing attitudes, we act. These actions, or karma, leave imprints on the continuity of our minds (mindstreams). The karmic imprints or potentials are like residual energy remaining after we've finished an action. Intangible, they are carried along by our mindstreams. When the environment is conducive, certain karmic potentials mature and bring forth our experiences.

This process is complex and generally takes time to understand fully. What follows is a brief description to give you a general idea.

From a Buddhist perspective, our minds are presently obscured by ignorance: we don't understand who we are in the deepest sense, or the mode in which people and phenomena exist. Unaware of our ultimate nature, we misconceive ourselves to be solid, real, findable people. This misconception of the self is apparent when we experience a strong emotion. For example, when we're angry, we feel there's a real I who is justifiably irate. But if we ask ourselves, "Who is angry?" we have a hard time pointing to exactly who this seemingly independent self is. In fact, our self or "I" exists, but not in the way we think it does.

We seek to protect and please this independent self, which is a creation of our misconceptions. Thus, we become attached to whatever gives us pleasure and have aversion towards the people and things that interfere with our happiness. From this ignorant view of ourselves springs jealousy, pride, closed-mindedness, grudge-holding, laziness and an assortment of other undesirable personality characteristics. These disturbing attitudes obscure our good qualities and prevent us from being the kind of people we would like to be.

Motivated by these disturbing attitudes, we act. "Karma" refers to the intentional actions of our body, speech and mind: what we think, say and do. Our actions stem from our minds. First a motivation arises in our minds, then we act. Sometimes, we're unaware of our motivations and are surprised at what we do and say. But if we're attentive, we'll observe that all our actions are preceded by motivations.

For example, before we criticize someone, the thought arises, "This person is making me unhappy. I want him to stop." Then we speak angrily, telling the other his defects. The Buddha explained that this action leaves an imprint on our mindstream, and later, when the external situation in our lives is conducive, this karmic potential matures and determines our experience.

Just as a small seed can grow into a tree with many fruits, this one action can produce several results: others will criticize us, our environment will be inhospitable, we'll habitually criticize others, and we'll have unfortunate rebirths.

Similarly, when we have good motivations, ones which are unselfish and concerned with others' benefit, we act constructively. This leaves positive imprints on our consciousness. These positive imprints likewise give rise to results: others will like us, our habitat will be pleasant, we'll have good personalities and will have fortunate rebirths.

Thus, at different times, we generate both disturbing attitudes and emotions such an anger, attachment and closed-mindedness, and positive emotions and attitudes such as love, self-respect, consideration for others and wisdom. The Buddhist path is one of eliminating the former attitudes and increasing the latter, to bring us and those around us more happiness.


## Taking Rebirth

Through his deep insight into how things exist, the Buddha observed that disturbing attitudes and karma cause our minds to take one rebirth after another. At the time of death, we ordinary beings crave for our bodies. We're afraid to lose our bodies and to be separated from everything around us. When it becomes obvious that we're departing from this body and life, we grasp for another body.

These two — craving and grasping — act as the cooperative conditions for karmic imprints to ripen at the time of death. As these karmic imprints start to mature, our minds are attracted to other bodies and we seek to take rebirth in them. In the case of a human rebirth, after passing through an intermediate state between one life and the next, our consciousness then enters a fertilized egg. We develop the aggregates of a human being — a human body and mind.

In this new rebirth, we perceive people and things through our senses. Experiencing pleasant or unpleasant feelings from them, we generate attachment, aversion or indifference. These motivations cause us to act. Our actions leave more imprints on our mindstreams, and at the time of death, we're again propelled to take rebirth in another body.

This cycle of rebirth is called *samsara*. *Samsara* isn't a place: it isn't our world. Rather, *samsara* — also called cyclic existence — is our situation of taking one rebirth after another under the control of disturbing attitudes and karmic actions.

Thus, our own energy causes us to be reborn who we are, in our present circumstance. However, karma isn't "cast in concrete," and our lives aren't predetermined. Which karmic imprints ripen depends on our environment and our state of mind. In addition, we have the ability to control our actions, and thus shape our future.

This is the law of karma, which is the functioning of cause and effect within our mindstreams. Whether we experience pain or pleasure depends on what we have done in the past. Our previous actions or karma were motivated by our minds. In this way, our minds are the principal creator of our experience.

## Was There a Beginning?

Some people wonder, "How did this process start? Was there a beginning to our universe and the beings in it?"

The physical evolution of our universe is a matter for scientific research. Science examines the continuity of physical material in our universe — how cause and effect operate physically to produce the various things in our universe.

Matter in our universe has a cause: a previous moment of matter or energy. It would be difficult to prove there was a time when neither matter nor energy existed. If there once was nothing, then out of what did matter arise? How could things be produced without causes? Our present universe is a transformation of the physical energy that existed previously.

Our mind isn't made of physical material and therefore its causes aren't material. Our mind arises from the previous moment of mind in its continuity. We can trace our consciousness back moment by moment to childhood. Our mind has changed since then, but our present mind is related to and caused by our mind when we were younger.

In this way, the existence of our mindstream can be traced back to the time of conception. The consciousness that entered the fertilized egg in our mother's womb must also have had a cause. From a Buddhist perspective, this is a previous moment of mind, i.e. our consciousness of a previous life. This continuity of mind goes back infinitely. There was no beginning. Just as the mathematical numberline has no beginning — one more can always be added — neither has the continuity of our consciousness.

Our disturbing attitudes, which include ignorance, also arise from causes: the previous moments of disturbing attitudes. Their continuity goes back infinitely. If there were a first moment of disturbing attitudes, then we should be able to point to what caused it. If we were initially pure and later became ignorant, where did ignorance come from? It's impossible for pure beings who perceive reality to later become ignorant. If someone becomes ignorant, he or she wasn't completely pure before.

Nor can another being make us ignorant. No one can put ignorance into our mindstreams the way water is poured into a cup.

From a Buddhist point of view, it's senseless to search for the beginning of our existence and the start of our disturbing attitudes. The Buddha was extremely practical, stressing that we deal with the present situation and try to remedy it. Getting lost in useless speculation prevents us from focusing on the present and improving it.

For example, a person is hit by a car and lies bleeding in the street. Before he'll accept medical attention, he insists on knowing who was driving the car, who manufactured it, and when it was made.

While seeking this information, he dies. We would say such a person is foolish. Knowing the origin of the car doesn't change his injury. Nor does it save his life. He would have been wiser to deal with his present situation, get medical attention and recover.

Similarly, it's better to examine our present difficulties and their cause — disturbing attitudes — and remedy them, rather than to get lost in speculation about a non-existent beginning. The Buddha didn't discuss the origin of the universe, because knowing that doesn't help us solve our problems or improve the quality of our lives. Instead, he explained how our minds cause our experience through motivating us to act (create karma). Understanding this enables us to gain control over and purify this process.


## Mind as the Interpreter of Our Environment

The second way in which our minds create our experience is by interpreting the objects we perceive. How we interpret something determines how we experience it. Although we generally assume we accurately perceive what is "out there," our experiences are in fact colored by our interpretations and projections.

For example, when two people meet Joe, one likes him while the other doesn't. One sees Joe as considerate and intelligent, someone with a good sense of humor. The other perceives Joe as a person who makes fun of others, and is competitive and insensitive to their feelings. Both assume they perceive Joe as he is. However, if that were true, they would perceive him the same way, and they clearly don't.

Both people hear the same words when Joe speaks, yet they interpret what is said differently. Their minds move very quickly from perception — the sounds and sights they perceive through their senses — to conclusion — the meaning given to the sense data.

Thus, one person experiences Joe's jokes as humorous and good-natured and thinks, "Joe is a nice person. I enjoy being with him." Thereafter, whenever he meets Joe, he sees a friend and expects to have a good time. The other interprets Joe's words as sarcastic and thinks, "Joe is egotistical. I don't like him." Later, when she meets him, she sees a disagreeable person and feels aversion.

Both people assume their perception of Joe is correct. But in fact, both relate to Joe through the veils of their own preconceptions. Joe's qualities of being friendly or obnoxious are created by the projections of the people perceiving him. In and of himself, Joe is neither.

How we look at a situation determines our experience of it. We may look at our mother and think, "She always tells me what to do. She's so demanding." Then every time we see her, we feel uncomfortable.

On the other hand, we may think, "My mother gave me this body. She took care of me when I was a helpless infant and couldn't even feed myself. She taught me how to speak and behave." Then our mother appears very kind to us. When we see her, she seems loving and we have affection for her.

Because we interpret certain behavior in others as harmful, we give them the label "enemies." Thereafter, they appear to us as enemies. Similarly, because we label other persons' behavior as kind and call them friends, that's how they appear to us. Friends and enemies actually come from our own minds. We create them. Having created our friends and enemies through the power of our minds, we then cling to our friends and try to harm our enemies. In fact, we're attached to or have aversion for what our own minds have created.

How we interpret our environment and the people in it depends on the purity of our minds. Just as the image reflected in a dirty mirror is unattractive and obscured, so too is the appearance of an object to a mind sullied by disturbing attitudes and negative karmic imprints. The same object reflected in a spotless mirror is clear and beautiful. Likewise, whatever is perceived by a pure mind is lovely.

Some mentally ill people believe the people around them are plotting to harm them. Overwhelmed by their fear, they may even see ghosts where there are none. Although they are convinced their perceptions are correct, we experience the same environment in a completely different way. This is due to the different actions we've done in the past as well as to the present functioning of our disturbing attitudes.

For a person advanced on the path to enlightenment, this earth is a pure land. For people whose minds are filled with anger, it's a fearful, hellish place. The environment doesn't exist as pleasurable or painful in and of itself. Our experience of it depends on our previously created actions and our present interpretations. Both hellish environments and pure lands are created by our minds. Our minds are the source, the creator, of our experience.

Knowing this, we become aware that the only way to arrive at a state of lasting and perfect happiness is to purify our minds of their disturbing attitudes and the imprints and stains of our karma. We're responsible, we can do this. A modern Buddhist hymn based on a verse from The *Dhammapada* says:

> By ourselves is evil done,
> By ourselves we pain endure.
> By ourselves we cease from wrong
> By ourselves we become pure
> No one saves us but ourselves
> No one can and no one may.
> We ourselves must walk the path,
> Buddhas merely show the way.

The Buddhas show us the path to follow. They know it because they have experienced it themselves. Those beings who are now Buddhas were once entrenched in their confusion and difficulties like we are now. However, by following the path, they purified their minds and developed their good qualities to the utmost, thereby becoming fully enlightened Buddhas. We have the potential to do the same.

The Buddhas guide us, but we must do the work. Just as our teachers can instruct us in grammar, but can't learn it for us, so too can the Buddhas give us teachings and guidance, but we must put them into practice. In the *White Lotus of the Holy Dharma Sutra*, it says:

> The Buddhas cannot wash away beings' negativities with water,
> They cannot remove beings' suffering with their hands,
> Nor can they transplant their realizations into others.
> The Buddhas liberate beings by teaching them the truth of thusness (emptiness).

While Buddhism emphasizes self-responsibility, that doesn't mean we are alone on the path. We can rely on the guidance, inspiration and example of the Three Jewels: the Buddhas, Dharma and Sangha.

The Buddhas are those beings who have purified all anger, attachment, ignorance and selfishness from their minds. In addition, they have developed all good qualities such as impartial love, compassion and wisdom.

The Dharma is the realizations of reality and the cessations of problems and sufferings caused by ignorance. In a general sense, the Dharma also refers to the Buddha's teachings which lead us to gain realizations.

Sangha refers to anyone who has realized reality, or selflessness, the absence of an independently-existing self. These people, who are well along the path to liberation and enlightenment, may be ordained (monks or nuns) or lay people. In a more general sense, the Sangha is the community of monks and nuns who have dedicated their lives to improving themselves and benefiting others.

In the upcoming chapters, we'll examine in greater depth how our minds create our experience. We'll also see how to tame the monkey mind — that unmanageable part of ourselves — so we can create the cause for happiness, make our lives meaningful, and have harmonious relationships with others.

# THE FOUR NOBLE TRUTHS

*Creatively dealing with difficulties*

The essence of the Buddha's teachings is expressed in the four noble truths. The first two truths are an accurate description of our present situation, and the last two show a practical way to improve it. We can validate the four noble truths through our own experience: a mystical leap of faith is not necessary.

These four facts are called noble because they are taught by the noble ones — those beings who have direct perception of reality. Also, by understanding these four, we'll be ennobled. They are truths because they are correct: it's true that sufferings and their causes are to be abandoned, and it's true that the cessation of sufferings and their causes and the path to attain this are to be adopted. These facts don't deceive us or lead us away from happiness. By understanding them, we'll enter the path to liberation and enlightenment.

The four noble truths are:

1. Suffering exists
2. Suffering has causes
3. Suffering can be eliminated
4. There is a true path to the cessation of suffering

Sufferings are to be identified; their causes are to be abandoned; the cessation of sufferings is to be realized; and the path is to be relied upon.

## The First Truth: Suffering Exists

The Pali and Sanskrit word *dukkha* is often translated as suffering. However, this English word is misleading because it connotes extreme pain. Thus some people falsely say, "My life is okay, I have no great problems. Why does Buddhism insist that life is suffering when in fact I experience much pleasure? Buddhism seems pessimistic!"

When the Buddha described our lives as *dukkha*, he was referring to any and all unsatisfactory conditions. These range from minor disappointments, problems and difficulties to intense pain and misery. Therefore, throughout this book all these words will be used to indicate *dukkha*, the fact that things aren't completely right in our lives and could be better.

Although initially we may not like to think about unsatisfactory conditions in our lives, it's necessary to do so in order to remedy them. For example, if someone is sick, but refuses to acknowledge it, she won't seek medication and thus won't recover. Similarly, if we pretend everything in our lives is fine, we won't look deeply to find the source of uneasiness and fear inside us. Without doing this, we can't eliminate it and reach a state of lasting happiness.

However, if we examine our situation clearly and acknowledge it, we'll be able to improve it. In addition, being honest with ourselves brings a sense of relief and hope, for we know our problems aren't insurmountable.

The Buddha described three types of problems or sufferings we face:

1. the suffering of pain
2. the suffering of change
3. pervasive compounded suffering

The suffering of pain occurs whenever we're mentally or physically miserable. Physical suffering includes headaches and scraped knees as well as the torment of cancer and heart attacks. Mental suffering occurs when we fail to get what we want, when we lose something we're attached to, or when misfortune comes our way. We're sad when our career goals cannot be achieved, we're depressed when we part from loved ones, we're anxious when the stock market goes down.

Mental and physical difficulties come to every living being, no matter where he or she lives. Technological progress may have eliminated many of our physical problems, but it also has created new ones such as pollution and the threat of nuclear war. We may have a higher living standard than ever before, but we also have more crime, increased drug abuse and a rise in suicide and divorce rates. Technology alone hasn't solved all our problems.

The suffering of change indicates that activities we generally regard as pleasurable in fact inevitably change and become painful. Consider food, for example. We regard eating delicious food as a source of pleasure. If this were true, then the more we ate, the happier we would be. This obviously isn't the case. While eating initially eliminates the pain of hunger, continuous eating brings on indigestion.

Similarly, we regard our friends as a source of pleasure. However, if pleasure intrinsically existed in being with our friends, then the more we were with them, the happier we would be. When we first see our friends, we're delighted and the pain of loneliness vanishes. But if they stay too long, we get tired and wish they would leave.

Although the objects and people around us give us some pleasure, too much of them makes us uncomfortable. The happiness we initially derive from them turns into unhappiness. This indicates that happiness was never inherent in those activities, objects or people, but was a product of the interaction between us and them.

Pervasive compounded suffering refers to our situation of having bodies and minds prone to pain. We can become miserable simply by the changing of external conditions. The weather changes and our bodies suffer from the cold; how a friend treats us changes and we become depressed.

This is called pervasive suffering because our present bodies and minds are pervaded with the potential to experience pain. We have no foolproof way to protect ourselves from it. It's also called pervasive suffering because this unsatisfactory state afflicts all beings who haven't realized the reality of how people and phenomena exist. Even those people who seem to have all the pleasures life could offer still become old and die.

Our present bodies and minds compound our misery in the sense that they're the basis for our present problems. Our present bodies are the basis upon which we experience bad health. If we didn't have a body that was receptive to pain, we wouldn't fall ill no matter how many viruses and germs we were exposed to. Similarly, our present minds are the basis upon which we experience the pain of hurt feelings. If we had minds that weren't contaminated by anger, then we wouldn't suffer from the mental anguish of conflict with others.

By being attached to our present bodies and minds, we act in ways that bring us more pain and confusion in the future. For example, to pamper our bodies, we may take others' things. Not only does this harm others, but it also leaves imprints in our own mindstreams which cause us to be deprived of possessions in the future.

Some people may feel forlorn after considering these three types of suffering, for it seems we're in a terrible situation. They may think Buddhism is unduly pessimistic for talking so much about suffering. However, if we understand the purpose of the Buddha's teachings, such misconceptions won't arise, and instead we'll feel inspired.

The reason for thinking about the unsatisfactory state we're in is to generate within ourselves the determination to be free from it and to have lasting happiness in its place. With this earnest intention to improve our lives, we'll investigate the causes of our problems and apply methods to eliminate them. This gives our lives profound meaning and clear direction.

## The Second Truth: Suffering Has Causes

As explained in the previous chapter, our minds are the source of our happiness and suffering. When we have wisdom and compassion, happiness follows; when we're confused by our disturbing attitudes, difficulties beset us. Therefore, it's important to differentiate between constructive and destructive states of mind so that we can increase the former and diminish the latter.

The chief cause of our problems is ignorance. Ignorance is a mental factor, or attitude, that obscures our understanding of who we are, and the mode in which all phenomena exist. Not only does ignorance prevent us from realizing how things exist, it also depicts things as existing in a way they do not.

For example, functioning things — things produced by causes and conditions, like a mountain, a pen, and our bodies — constantly change moment by moment. Under the influence of ignorance, however, we treat them as if they were unchanging and static. Thus, when we meet a friend we haven't seen for a long time, we're startled by how much she has aged. Similarly, we're surprised when things break, for although we may intellectually know they change, in our hearts we still believe they are static. Although scientists tell us sub-atomic substances are in constant motion, when we look at a table, it appears solid and unchanging to us. Ignorance makes our perceptions not accord with reality.

A deeper level of ignorance is what Buddhists call the misconception of inherent existence. Many books have been written on this subject, and it takes time to get a good understanding of it. The misconception of inherent existence is identified as the root of all our disturbing attitudes and problems. Its remedy, the wisdom realizing emptiness or reality, is thus the heart of Buddhist teachings.

Inherent existence means that people and phenomena appear to us as if they exist in and of themselves, with an essential nature making them what they are. For example, a flower is composed of many parts — a stem, petals, stamen and pistils. However, the flower appears to us as a single phenomena with something in it that makes it inherently a flower.

Similarly, each person is composed of a body and a mind, and on that basis is given his or her name. However, when we look at someone, there appears to be a "real" person, someone who exists independently of his or her body and mind, independently of his or her name. Things falsely appear to be inherently existent, and we ignorantly assent to this appearance and grasp or conceive them to exist independently. Whereas everything exists dependently, we innately conceive it to be independent.

This ignorance of the ultimate nature — that everything is empty of independent or inherent existence — is the root from which grow our other disturbing attitudes. It impacts our daily lives by making us attached to whatever seems pleasurable and angry at whatever is displeasing. Under the influence of attachment and aversion, our moods roller coaster from high to low each day.

Attachment overestimates the good qualities of a person or thing and then clings to it. Anger exaggerates the negative qualities of a person or thing and wants to harm it. Disturbed by attachment and anger, most people — and animals too — spend their lives helping their friends and harming their enemies. Besides these three principal poisons — ignorance, attachment and anger — others influence us as well: jealousy, pride, laziness, grudge-holding and so on.

In daily life, these disturbing attitudes influence our actions. For example, attachment to our own personal success may make us compete, rather than cooperate, with our colleagues at work. Anger impels us to lose our temper and insult others. We need only reflect on our actions, read the newspaper or turn on the TV to see what attachment and anger cause people to do.

These actions, or karma, leave imprints on our mindstreams. As explained before, the imprints propel us to take rebirth and to experience unsatisfactory conditions wherever we're born.

Even positive actions, such as helping someone out of love, will bring only short-term happiness in the future as long as we're still influenced by ignorance. Lasting happiness comes only when all ignorance is removed. Thus, these two factors — disturbing attitudes and karma — are the causes of our constantly recurring problems.

## The Third Truth: Suffering Can Be Eliminated

The disturbing attitudes and karma can be eliminated. They aren't the intrinsic nature of our minds. Since the disturbing attitudes arise from the misconception of ignorance, once we realize emptiness, or the nature of things as they are, ignorance no longer influences us. It's like turning a light on in a room: the darkness vanishes.

Through wisdom, we can cleanse ignorance and other disturbing attitudes from our mindstreams forever. Thus, we'll stop doing actions that propel us to take rebirth. In addition, wisdom cleanses the karmic imprints currently on our mindstreams, so they won't bring results.

Cessation is the lack of, or the stopping of, a certain disturbing attitude. A cessation is a negative phenomenon, i.e., it's an absence of a disturbing attitude. As we progress along the path and gradually eliminate the disturbing attitudes, the gross levels and then the subtle levels of anger, attachment and ignorance will cease. When we've eliminated all disturbing attitudes from their roots, we'll attain nirvana or liberation, the cessation of all suffering and all causes of suffering. In *The Dhammapada*, the Buddha said:

Just as a rowboat is lightened
When you bail all the water out,
So too nirvana is attained
When hate and greed are given up.

Nirvana is a blissful state in which we'll no longer take rebirth under the influence of disturbing attitudes and karma. After death, people who have attained liberation single-pointedly meditate on reality the emptiness of inherent existence — and thus abide in peace, with unceasing happiness.

People seeking self-liberation from cyclic existence are either called hearers or solitary-realizers. The hearers are so called because they hear and teach the Buddha's doctrine. The solitary realizers, in their last lifetime, attain nirvana in solitude, at a time when a Buddha isn't present. Hearers and solitary realizers who attain nirvana are called arhats, or foe destroyers, because they have destroyed the foe of disturbing attitudes.

Some people prefer to follow the bodhisattva path, aiming to become Buddhas in order to benefit all others. Even after they have ceased all their own disturbing attitudes and karma, bodhisattvas deliberately take rebirth in cyclic existence to guide and teach others. Their rebirths are motivated by compassion, not ignorance. Thus, they remain in the world to work for others.

While acting for the benefit of others, bodhisattvas work to eliminate the subtle stains on their own mindstreams so they can become fully enlightened Buddhas. Although bodhisattvas have such strong love and compassion for others that they vow not to attain enlightenment until they've led all beings to enlightenment, in actual fact, these bodhisattvas don't forsake their own enlightenment. The significance of their vow is that if it were beneficial for others, they would gladly forsake their own liberation. However, because they realize they'll be more efficacious in helping others as a Buddha, they actively seek enlightenment. Once they become Buddhas, they still manifest in the world to guide others.

Buddhahood, or full enlightenment, is a step beyond the lofty attainments of arhats. One way to distinguish the two is according to the level of obscurations removed from their minds.

There are two levels of obscurations: the deluded obscurations, which are disturbing attitudes and karma, and the obscurations to all-knowing, which are the appearance of phenomena as inherently existent and the inability to directly perceive all phenomena simultaneously. The two levels of obscurations are analogous to onions in a pot and the smell remaining once the onions have been removed. When the deluded obscurations have been removed, one attains liberation or arhatship. If one continues to purify the mind, removing the obscurations to all-knowing, then one attains the complete enlightenment of a Buddha.

Because a bodhisattva aspires to help others in the most effective and extensive way, he or she meditates to purify both obscurations. While lower-level bodhisattvas still have deluded obscurations, the higher bodhisattvas have eliminated them and are in the process of removing their obscurations to all-knowing. When a bodhisattva becomes a Buddha, he or she can then manifest in the world in whatever ways are necessary to lead others to enlightenment.

Some people become arhats first before becoming Buddhas, while others enter directly into the bodhisattva path. The former generate the firm determination to be free from cyclic existence, thereby entering the path of the hearers or solitary realizers. After attaining nirvana, they abide in a state of bliss. Later on, they cultivate the altruistic intention to attain enlightenment in order to benefit others. At this time, they enter the bodhisattva path and later attain Buddhahood.

Other people cultivate the determination to be free and the altruistic intention initially. When both of these are firm, they enter the bodhisattva path directly without first becoming arhats. At the end of the bodhisattva path, they too become Buddhas.

## The Fourth Truth: a True Path to the Cessation of Suffering

Full cessation is the absence or stopping of suffering and its causes. To arrive at this freedom, we must follow the correct path. In the

*Mahaparinirvana Sutra* and in many other sutras, the Buddha described the path to nirvana as the three higher trainings — ethics, concentration and wisdom. He also enumerated the noble eightfold path, which can be subsumed in the three higher trainings.

### The Higher Training in Ethics *(Sila)*

The higher training in ethics is the foundation of the practice. Through it, we cease doing negative actions that eventually cause us pain.

---

## THE FOUR NOBLE TRUTHS AND
## THE NOBLE EIGHTFOLD PATH

1. True sufferings (unsatisfactory experiences)
2. True causes of these experiences
   - Disturbing attitudes
   - Karmic actions
3. True cessations of unsatisfactory experiences and their causes
4. True paths to peace
   - Higher training in ethics
     1. Correct action
     2. Correct speech
     3. Correct livelihood
   - Higher training in concentration
     4. Correct effort
     5. Correct mindfulness
     6. Correct concentration
   - Higher training in wisdom
     7. Correct view
     8. Correct realization

---

Ethics is very practical for it improves the quality of our daily lives. As we cease harming others, our regret and guilt will subside. In addition, others will trust us and will be attracted to us. We'll die peacefully, free from fear of being reborn in bad circumstances. All the positive potential (merit) we create by abandoning destructive actions and creating positive ones sets a firm foundation for all future realizations of the path.

Three branches of the noble eightfold path are included in the higher training in ethics. Although they are briefly explained below, their meanings become clearer when we reflect on them by making examples from our lives.

**1. Right action.** Acting properly, we can avoid creating the three destructive actions of the body: killing, stealing and unwise sexual behavior.

Killing is intentionally taking the life of any being, including animals. The advice to avoid killing challenges us to think creatively of alternate means to resolve conflict besides violence.

Stealing is taking what isn't given to us. It includes not paying taxes or fees that are due, borrowing things and not returning them, and taking things from our workplace for our own personal use.

Unwise sexual behavior refers chiefly to adultery, but there are other branches are well. This is elaborated in a later chapter.

Right action teaches us to be aware of the effects of our actions on others. Instead of doing whatever pleases us at the moment, we'll be considerate of others. Automatically, our relationships will improve and others will be happier in our company.

Right action also includes physically acting in ways that benefit others. This includes helping an elderly person to clean house, saving others' lives by rescuing them from danger and so on.

**2. Right speech.** Right speech begins with avoiding four destructive actions of speech: lying, divisive words, harsh words and idle talk.

Lying is verbally saying or indicating through a nod or a shrug something we know isn't true. However, telling the truth should be tempered with compassion. For instance, it isn't wise to tell the truth to a murderer about a potential victim's whereabouts, if this would cause the latter's death.

Using divisive words is to cause others to quarrel or to prevent them from becoming harmonious once they've had a falling out.

Harsh words hurt others. This includes insult, abuse, ridicule, sarcasm and so on. Sometimes harsh words can be said with a smile, as when we innocently pretend what we have said won't hurt another.

Idly talking about inconsequential topics only for amusement wastes our time and others' time.

Through training in right speech we'll communicate in ways pleasing to others. Our relationships with other people will be more fulfilling if we take care of what we say to them and how we say it. Rather than venting our anger or frustration onto another, we'll think about effective ways to communicate our needs and feelings to them. In addition, we'll make an effort to notice and comment upon others' good qualities and achievements. We'll give others moral support, console them in times of grief, and teach them the Dharma. Speech is a powerful tool to influence others and if we use it wisely, many people will benefit.

The Buddha advised us to avoid ten destructive actions: three physical, four verbal and three mental. The three physical actions were discussed under right action and the four verbal under right speech. Avoiding the three destructive actions of mind — coveting, maliciousness and wrong views — aren't specifically mentioned under the higher training in ethics, but they'll be discussed here because avoiding them helps us to live ethically.

Coveting others' possessions is when we plan how to procure something belonging to another person. While coveting is a mental action no one else can see, it can lead us to flatter, bribe, cheat or steal from others to obtain what we desire.

Maliciousness is planning to harm others. It includes thinking how to revenge a wrong done to us, how to hurt others' feelings or how to embarrass them.

Holding wrong views involves vigorously and hostilely denying the existence of such things as past and future lives, the possibility of attaining nirvana, the existence of the Buddhas, Dharma and Sangha. Doubt about these subjects does not constitute wrong views. However, if we neglect to resolve our doubts by asking questions and investigating these issues, we could later generate wrong views by believing in deceptive doctrines.

By deliberately refraining from these ten destructive actions, we engage in the ten constructive or positive actions. For example, deciding not to lie to our employer about the time spent working on a project is in itself a positive action. This has many benefits: our employer will trust our word in the future, we will live according to our ethical principles, and we will create the cause to have temporal happiness and spiritual realizations.

**3. Right livelihood.** Material possessions are needed to sustain our lives, but it's important to procure them in proper ways. It's detrimental to engage in any of the physical or verbal negative actions to earn a living, nor should we cause others to do so. Therefore, the Buddha recommended that we avoid being a butcher, hunter or soldier. We should also avoid jobs that entail selling liquor, gambling, dealing in livestock, animal skins or pesticides; manufacturing or selling weapons; usury or fraud.

Some people may wonder for example, how people could eat if there were no butchers or if no pesticides were used on crops. The important point here is we ourselves shouldn't engage in wrong livelihood. We can't control what other people do, nor can we alone decide our country's policies. When there is a choice, we should select a profession that doesn't harm others. When there is no choice, then we must do the best we can, given the situation. The most important factor is to abandon the wish to harm others.

For ordained people, right livelihood means keeping their precepts, thereby being worthy of offerings made to them. If an ordained person deceives or cheats others, tells fortunes or performs magic to earn money, it is wrong livelihood. Everyone — ordained or lay — should play a useful role in society and not harm others to live.

The various sets of precepts set out by the Buddha are included in the higher training of ethics. They are described in the chapter entitled "Precepts."

### The Higher Training in Concentration (*Samadhi*)

Concentration is an essential part of the path, for without it our minds are unable to remain firmly on virtuous objects. For example, when we meditate on love, we must first generate that attitude and then maintain it. In that way, it will be fully integrated in our minds. When we meditate on emptiness, we must first penetrate its meaning and then sustain that understanding. Transforming our minds through meditation is possible only when we can stop uncontrolled distracting thoughts.

The higher training in concentration leads to calm abiding (*samatha*), the ability to hold our concentration on the meditation object for as long as we wish. In the process of developing calm abiding, a practitioner chooses one particular meditation object, for example the breath or the image of the Buddha. Once calm abiding is attained, concentration can be directed at any object: emptiness, love etc. With calm abiding, the mind and the body are extremely pliant, making meditation very easy and enjoyable.

The next three branches of the noble eightfold path are included in the higher training of concentration:

**4. Right effort.** To progress on the path, we need to put our energy into Dharma practice. With enthusiastic effort, we can purify negative actions already done and prevent doing new ones in the future. Effort also is necessary to maintain the virtuous states we've already generated and to induce new ones in the future. Doing this definitely improves the quality of our lives.

**5. Right mindfulness.** Mindfulness is a mental factor that enables us to remember and to keep our attention on what is beneficial. For example, in the morning when we awake, we can determine, "Today I will try not to harm others and to benefit them as much as possible." Mindfulness enables us to keep this thought in our minds all day and makes us aware whether or not our daily actions correspond to this motivation. Being mindful of the ten constructive actions enables us not to lie, steal and so forth when we're tempted to do so.

Mindfulness is also important in meditation. Meditation means familiarizing ourselves with a beneficial object or attitude. For example, we may focus our attention on our breath as we inhale and exhale. This clears the flurry of thoughts from our minds, and eventually, we'll be able to concentrate single-pointedly on the breath. The meditation object may vary: in some meditations, we may focus on the breath, in others on the visualized image of the Buddha or on loving-kindness for all beings.

To develop single-pointed concentration or *samadhi*, we must eliminate all opposing states of mind such as forgetfulness, laxity and agitation.

Forgetfulness prevents us from maintaining our object of meditation — the breath, the image of the Buddha, the kindness of other beings and so on. We forget the object of meditation and are distracted by the flurry of thoughts in our minds.

Laxity occurs when the mind is dull and its clarity or attentiveness decreases. If we don't oppose gross laxity, we may fall asleep on our meditation cushion. If we neglect to remedy subtle laxity, we may wrongly believe we've attained a high level of concentration when we haven't.

Agitation interrupts the stability of our concentration. It distracts us from the meditation object by diverting our attention to something we're attached to. For example, we may be trying to meditate when we find that our attention has drifted to food. Suddenly the bell rings to end the meditation session, and we realize we haven't meditated at all!

Mindfulness counteracts these hindrances. It is a mental factor that repeatedly returns our attention to a familiar object, in this case the meditation object — the breath, etc. It's important to learn how to meditate. Then, our mindfulness will be strong, and we won't forget the meditation object as easily. If we do, our introspective alertness will warn us that we're distracted. Renewing our mindfulness, we'll again bring our attention back to the meditation object.

Mindfulness makes our concentration stable, thus counteracting agitation. It also enables our minds to be clear and attentive, thus eliminating laxity. Through experimentation, we must find the correct balance between making our concentration too tight or too loose. Tightness causes agitation, and this disturbs the stability of our concentration. Loose attention brings laxity and disturbs the clarity and attentiveness of the mind. The balance between making our attention too loose or too tight is like fine-tuning a violin. The Indian meditator and sage Chandragomin said:

If we do not make the effort to build intensive attention, the mind will begin to sink and we will never be able to achieve clarity. On the other hand, if we place too much emphasis on maintaining intensive attention, this causes the mind to wander from the object and we will never be able to achieve stability. Hence it is not easy to keep to the middle way when developing a single-pointed mind.

In addition to employing the mental factor of mindfulness as an essential aid in developing concentration, the Buddha also spoke of cultivating mindfulness of four objects: our bodies, feelings, minds, and phenomena. Through this practice, we're able to realize three characteristics: that everything is constantly changing, that all things under the influence of disturbing thoughts and karma are unsatisfactory, and that all phenomena are selfless.

**6. Right concentration.** Our concentration or single-pointedness slowly improves through effort and mindfulness, until we attain calm abiding. We may also progress to deeper states of concentration, the actual meditative stabilizations (*jhana, dhyana*) of the form and formless realms.

These levels of meditative stabilization are cultivated by non-Buddhists as well. However, when a Buddhist cultivates them, his or her mind is sustained by refuge in the Three Jewels (the Buddhas, Dharma and Sangha), and by the determination to be free of all sufferings of cyclic existence. Whereas non-Buddhists tend to be satisfied with the bliss of the various meditative stabilizations, Buddhists employ the meditative stabilizations to realize emptiness, thereby attaining liberation.

The Buddha gave extensive teachings on mindfulness and concentration. If you're interested in learning more, ask a spiritual mentor for instruction or refer to books on the subject.

### The Higher Training in Wisdom (*Panna, Prajna*)

Through living ethically, we'll eliminate physical and verbal negative actions. By developing concentration, the manifest disturbing attitudes will temporarily subside. However, without wisdom, there is no way to liberate ourselves from cyclic existence and attain lasting happiness. To eradicate the cause of all problems — ignorance — from our mindstreams, the wisdom realizing emptiness (generally synonymous with selflessness or lack of an inherent self) is necessary.

To gain this wisdom which realizes the deeper nature of how people and phenomena exist, we must practice special insight (*vipassana*). Special insight is a discriminating wisdom conjoined with the pliancy of calm abiding, induced by the power of analysis.

Prior to the attainment of special insight, whenever we use analysis in meditation, our concentration is disturbed, and whenever the mind concentrates single-pointedly, it's unable to analyze simultaneously. However, when special insight is attained, concentration and analysis don't disturb each other, thereby making the mind very powerful. When special insight is directed towards selflessness, it cleanses our mindstreams of ignorance, disturbing attitudes, karma and their imprints so they never return.

To develop calm abiding and special insight, we must train for a long time. Like learning to read, developing concentration and wisdom takes time and continuous practice. In our modern times of push-button appliances and fast food, we tend to be impatient and expect to gain high realization without much effort. However, this isn't possible. A few people, who have cultivated the path extensively in previous lives, may make rapid progress this life. But for the majority of us, this isn't the case. Therefore, it's helpful if we have a long-range goal, patience, enthusiasm and a happy mind aspiring for what is good.

The last two branches of the noble eightfold path are included in the higher training of wisdom:

**7. Right view or understanding.** This is the understanding of the four noble truths: the truths of suffering and its causes perpetuate cyclic existence, the truths of cessation and the path are the way to liberation. Specifically, right view is the wisdom that opposes deluded views — such as the concept grasping our body-mind complex having an inherent self — which keep us bound in cyclic existence. This will be discussed more in depth in the chapter "The Far-reaching Attitudes", in the section entitled "Wisdom".

**8. Right thought.** Non-attachment, benevolence and non-harmfulness are the characteristics of right thought. On a deeper level, right thought refers to the mind that subtly analyzes emptiness, thus leading us to perceive it directly.

Although ethics, concentration and wisdom are generally described as a progressive path, they can be practiced simultaneously. Ethics and concentration are the basis to gain wisdom. Wisdom and concentration help our ethical conduct to be firm and well-motivated. Ethics gives our mind the strength to develop concentration, and wisdom lessens attachment, thereby reducing agitation and distraction. While we may direct most of our energies on one of the practices at any particular time, we shouldn't neglect any of them.

# FROM CONFUSION TO ENLIGHTENMENT:

*A step-by-step method to transform our minds*

The four noble truths and the noble eightfold path are one way to explain the path. The gradual path to enlightenment is another. These two ways are compatible. It's helpful for us to know them both, for by looking at the same thing from different perspectives, our understanding of it increases.

Since the Buddha taught a wide variety of audiences, beginners are sometimes confused about where to start and how to progress. Therefore, in the early 11th century, the Indian sage Atisha extracted the essential points from the sutras and ordered them into a gradual path. These are contained in his text, *Lamp of the Path*. The Tibetan sage, Lama Tzong Khapa (1357-1419) later expanded on the points in Atisha's text, and wrote *The Great Exposition on the Gradual Path to Enlightenment*.

The gradual path gives us an overview of the entire process of moving from confusion to enlightenment. It sets out in a clear manner the steps to realize the path. If we're familiar with these steps, then whenever we hear Dharma instructions we'll know to what level of the path they apply. By understanding the practices at different stages of the path, we'll realize there are no contradictions in the Buddha's teachings. They can all be included in one person's practice to reach enlightenment. Knowing this, we'll avoid the great fault of criticizing any Buddhist tradition or teaching. What follows is a summary of the gradual path to enlightenment.

## Precious Human Life

The first step of the path is understanding our present opportunity to practice the Dharma and to improve ourselves. If a beggar doesn't realize she has a jewel in her pocket, she won't make use of it and will remain poor. Similarly, if we don't understand our great opportunity, we won't use our time wisely.

Currently, we have precious human lives, endowed with many

qualities difficult to attain. Because of this, we can make our lives highly meaningful. We often take our lives for granted and dwell on the things that aren't going the way we would like them to. Thinking this way is unrealistic and makes us depressed. However, if we think about the freedom and qualities we do have and everything that is going well, we'll have a different and more joyful perspective on life.

One of our greatest endowments is our human intelligence. This precious quality enables us to investigate the meaning of life and to practice the path to enlightenment. If all of our senses — eyes, ears, mental — are intact, we are able to hear the Dharma, read books on it, and think about its meaning. We're born in an historical era when the Buddha has appeared and taught the Dharma. These teachings have been transmitted in a pure form from teacher to student in lineages stemming back to the Buddha. We have the opportunity to meet qualified spiritual masters who can teach us, and there are communities of ordained people and Dharma friends who share our interest and encourage us on the path.

Those of us who are fortunate to live in countries that cherish religious freedom aren't restricted from learning and practicing the path. In addition, most of us don't live in desperate poverty and thus have enough food, clothing and shelter to engage in spiritual practice without worrying about basic material needs. Our minds aren't heavily obscured with wrong views and we are interested in self-development.

We have the potential to do great things with our present opportunity. But to appreciate this, we must develop a long-term vision. Our present lives last only a short time. Our mindstreams don't cease when our physical bodies die. Our minds are formless entities, and when they leave our present bodies at the time of death, they will be reborn in other bodies. What rebirth we'll take depends on our present actions. Therefore, one purpose of our lives can be to prepare for death and future lives. In that way, we can die peacefully, knowing our minds will be propelled towards good rebirths.

The second way we can utilize our lives is to attain liberation or enlightenment. We can become arhats, beings liberated from cyclic existence, or we can go on to become fully enlightened Buddhas, able to benefit others most effectively. Attaining liberation, our minds will be completely cleansed of all disturbing attitudes. Thus we'll never become angry, jealous or proud again. We'll no longer feel guilty, anxious or depressed, and all our bad habits will be gone. In addition, if we aspire to attain enlightenment for the benefit of everyone, we'll have spontaneous affection for all beings, and will know the most appropriate ways to help them.

The third way to take advantage of our precious human lives is to live life to the fullest, moment by moment. There are several ways to do this. One is to be be mindful of each moment, being in the here-and-now as we act. When we eat, we concentrate on eating, noting the taste and texture of the food. When we walk, we concentrate on the movements involved in walking, without letting our minds wander to 101 other thoughts.

Another way to live each moment to the fullest is to practice thought transformation. For example, when we go upstairs, we can think, "May I lead all beings to fortunate rebirths, liberation and enlightenment." While washing dishes or clothes, we think, "May I help all beings cleanse their minds of disturbing attitudes and obscurations." When we hand something to another person, we think, "May I be able to satisfy the needs of all beings." We can creatively transform each action by generating the wish to bring happiness to others. Other techniques for making our daily lives meaningful are explained in the chapter, "Practical Guidelines for Good Living."

## Three Levels of Motivation

Having decided to make our lives meaningful, we can progress along the paths of the three levels of training. These correspond to the three levels of spiritual seekers. In *Lamp of the Path*, the great Indian sage Atisha said:

Those who fervently work by some means merely for happiness in cyclic existence are known as those of minimal spiritual motivation. Those who, having turned their backs on the pleasures of cyclic existence, and with a nature turned from negativities, fervently work for just their own serenity (liberation), are known as people of intermediate motivation. Those who fully wish to eliminate completely all the problems of others as they would the problems afflicting their own mindstreams are those of supreme spiritual motivation.

These three motivations and their corresponding trainings form the gradual path. The first level is the foundation for the second, which is the basis for the third. To progress along the path, we train serially, although we may aspire for full enlightenment throughout. These three motivations and their trainings in brief are:

1. The initial level. Here we want to prepare for death so we can die peacefully and attain a good rebirth. To this end, we'll contemplate impermanence, death and the disadvantages of unfortunate rebirths. At this point, our principal practice will be taking refuge in the Three Jewels and observing cause and effect (karma). Taking refuge is entrusting ourselves to the spiritual guidance of the Buddhas, Dharma and Sangha. Observing cause and effect entails trying to avoid the ten destructive actions and to act positively. Many of the practices of the higher training in ethics start at this point of the path.

2. The intermediate level. Here we seek to be completely free from the cyclic of rebirth. To this end, we'll contemplate the sufferings of cyclic existence in general and the problems of each type of rebirth in particular. We'll also consider the role of disturbing attitudes and karma in keeping us bound in cyclic existence. In this way, we'll generate a firm determination to be free from all difficulties of cyclic existence and to attain liberation. Our principal practice will be the three higher trainings, especially concentration and wisdom. All the branches of the noble eightfold path will be practiced as well.

3. The highest level. Here we seek liberation not only for ourselves, but for all beings. To do this, we must generate, the altruistic intention to attain enlightenment in order to benefit all beings(bodhicitta). Thus we'll meditate on great love, great compassion and altruism. Seeing the full enlightenment of the Buddhas as the best way to help others, we'll engage in the bodhisattvas' practice of the six far-reaching attitudes (perfections, *paramitas*): generosity, ethics, patience, joyous

effort, meditative stabilization and wisdom. The Vajrayana practice then enables us to attain the body and mind of a Buddha.

Let's now begin with the initial level to learn how to gradually transform our minds.

# THE GRADUAL PATH TO ENLIGHTENMENT

Included in true paths (the fourth noble truth) is gaining deep understanding of:
1. Our precious human life
2. The three levels of motivation
   - First level: looking beyond our present happiness to prepare for future lives
     1. Impermanence of life and death
     2. Danger of an unfortunate rebirth
     3. Taking refuge
     4. Karma: the law of cause and effect

   - Second level: seeking liberation from cyclic existence
     1. True sufferings and their causes are to be abandoned
     2. True cessations and the paths are to be adopted

   - Third level: seeking enlightenment for the benefit of all beings
     1. Developing the altruistic intention
        - Equanimity towards friends, enemies and strangers
        - Recognizing that all beings have been our mother
        - Remembering our mothers' kindness

- Wishing to repay it
- Love
- Compassion
- Great determination
- Altruistic intention
2. Practicing the bodhisattva's far-reaching attitudes
   - Generosity
   - Ethics
   - Patience
   - Joyous Effort
   - Meditative Stabilization
   - Wisdom
3. Vajrayana

# THE FIRST STEP:

*Looking beyond our present happiness*

## Remembering Death

The opportunity our precious human lives provide doesn't last forever. Death comes to everyone. Most people feel uncomfortable thinking about death, fearing that talking about death will bring it closer. However, by their very nature our lives are impermanent, and death is inevitable. Given that death is an irrevocable result of living, it's good to think about it to make our lives more meaningful.

Regarding death from a proper perspective can give us direction and energy to live fully. It's also a powerful tool for subduing our disturbing attitudes and making our minds peaceful, for when we recognize we'll inevitably die, all the petty concerns that worry us become insignificant compared to the importance of following the path before our lives end. The Buddha said:

> There is no greater realization than awareness of the impermanence of our lives. Just as the elephant's footprint is the biggest of all animals' footprints, so is meditation on impermanence the most powerful meditation.

At the time of death, our mindstreams and the imprints of the actions we've created go on to future lives. If we spend our precious human lives acting harmfully with bad motivations, the imprints of those actions will come with us. In addition, having reinforced our anger and jealousy and so on, they'll be stronger in future lives.

On the other hand, if we use our time wisely to cultivate positive states of mind — generosity, patience, love, compassion, concentration, wisdom — then the imprints from the actions they've motivated come with us. Also, those beneficial attitudes are stronger and can arise more easily in future lives. Thus, it's important to be concerned about what we think, say and do now.

Death definitely comes to everyone. Whether we're rich or poor, famous or humble, we'll die. No one can live forever for our bodies naturally decay and die. There is nowhere we can go to avoid death.

Our lifespans can't be extended and with every passing moment, they're becoming shorter. Death comes, whether or not we've taken the time to practice the path. When our lifespans run out, we can't bargain for more time in order to transform our minds. Truly realizing the certainty of death, we'll make a firm decision to practice the Dharma.

The time of death isn't certain. The duration of our lifespans isn't fixed, and even though statistics give a general indication of how long people live, that's not a guarantee about our own lives. It's incorrect to think we'll die when our life's work is complete, for people are always in the middle of doing something when they die: some people leave for vacation and don't return, some begin a meal and don't finish it.

Sustaining our lives takes great effort. If we simply did nothing, we'd naturally die. To stay alive, we have to arrange for food, shelter, clothing, medicine and other necessities. Even some things which are supposed to sustain life terminate it: for example, a house kills the people in it during an earthquake; bad food causes fatal illnesses. Our human bodies are very fragile. The skin is so easily penetrated, the bones so easy to break. Even tiny viruses cause the demise of huge humans. Deeply understanding the uncertainty of the time of death, we'll determine to practice the Dharma now, without procrastinating.

At the time of death, we must leave all our possessions behind. Although we spend our lives amassing things, not one of them can accompany us at death. Likewise, our friends and relatives can't come with us. Although we deeply care about them, in death there is no choice but to separate. Even our bodies, the one thing we've had since the beginning of this life, are left behind at the time of death. Just the karmic imprints accompany our mindstreams to future lives. Only our Dharma practice can benefit us in death. Genuinely understanding this, we'll determine to practice Dharma purely, without worldly motivations seeking wealth or reputation.

Does this mean Buddhists can't have fun and must live austerely? No, it doesn't. But, it does mean we ask ourselves, "What is really beneficial in life?" We must examine the motivations behind our actions and the results they'll bring in future lives. In this way, we can decide what is beneficial to do.

For example, if we cheat in business to increase our profits so our family can live in luxury, our motive is a selfish one. Although we want our relatives to be happy, we're placing their happiness above that of the people we're cheating. In fact, both parties want happiness and equally deserve a good life. If we act negatively, out of partiality for our own family, we harm others. Although our families may have a few extra possessions, at the time of death these stay behind, and the negative imprints we created by cheating others accompany us to future lives.

Understanding this, we'll see that the disadvantages of cheating outweigh its benefits, and we'll avoid doing it. Our families may have slightly fewer possessions, but we'll be able to sleep with a clear conscience. The positive action of deliberately avoiding cheating will bring us good results in the future.

Let's take another example: idle talk is usually considered a destructive action because it wastes our time. But if our friend is depressed and can't listen to wise advice, we can joke, tell silly stories and indulge in small talk to lighten his mood. Because our motivation is good, our joking and chatting are positive.

Laughing and having a good time aren't in opposition to Dharma. The more we leave behind attachment, anger, jealousy and pride, the more we'll enjoy whatever we're doing. Our hearts will open to others and we can laugh and smile with ease. The holy beings I've been fortunate to meet have a wonderful sense of humor and are very friendly.

In Buddhist groups, it's important for people to get to know each other and have a sense of fellowship. We can share experiences with our Dharma friends and encourage each other on the path. Buddhism isn't an isolated path, and Buddhists should cultivate group unity and companionship.

It's not beneficial to retreat inside ourselves thinking, "Every time I talk to someone I'm motivated by attachment. Therefore I'll concentrate on meditation and chanting and won't socialize with others." One of the fundamental principles of Buddhism is care and compassion for others. Although at times we may need to distance ourselves from others in order to settle our own minds, whenever possible we should actively develop genuine love for others. To do this, we must be aware of what's happening in others' lives, care about them as we do ourselves, and offer help whenever possible. Our ability to act with love develops with time and practice, and it has to be balanced with our need for private contemplation.

Buddhism isn't opposed to having material possessions, keeping our bodies healthy and attractive, or caring for our friends and relatives. Our possessions, body or dear ones don't enslave us. The real problem lies with our attachment, anger and other disturbing attitudes that arise in relationship to these things. If we're attached to material possessions, then we're likely to lie, cheat or steal to get them. Or we may stingily cling to our possessions, or use them selfishly to gain fame or to exert our power over others. This attachment binds us, affecting not only our relationships with others in the present, but how we'll be reborn in the future.

On the other hand, we can think, "I need certain possessions to sustain my life and my family. I'll work honestly to get them, and will share them with others and use them to spread the Dharma." With such a motivation, we'll live ethically and will create positive potential — positive karmic imprints on our minds — by being generous. In addition, we'll be more relaxed because we'll be free from miserliness.

## The Danger of an Unfortunate Rebirth

After death, where will we be reborn? From a Buddhist point of view, this depends upon our actions while alive and which imprints mature at the time of death. If we're angry at the time of death or if we cling strongly to our possessions and dear ones, that encourages the ripening of a negative imprint which will propel us towards a rebirth full of problems. If we die thinking of the Three Jewels or dedicating our lives for the benefit of others, that will help positive imprints to propel us towards fortunate rebirths.

In cyclic existence there are six life forms: the fortunate ones are gods, demi-gods and humans; and the unfortunate ones are animals, hungry ghosts and beings experiencing intense pain. It may seem strange to think that we can be born in these other life forms, but if we examine our minds, we'll see it's possible.

For example, sometimes we humans act and think like animals or even worse. We can be greedy, territorial, ferocious or dull-witted like some animals. While animals only kill to eat or to defend themselves, sometimes humans kill out of whim, spite or desire. If humans act like that, it seems natural that at the time of death their minds will be attracted towards bodies that match their mental states.

Unfortunate rebirths aren't punishments for acting badly. The compassionate Buddha didn't create these life forms, nor does he judge us and condemn us to them. These realms are created by our own minds and the imprints of our actions direct us towards them. The Indian sage Shantideva said:

> The immense fires and burning iron ground
> Of the beings experiencing intense pain
> Are not somebody's creation,
> But arise from the destructive thoughts within our minds.

> All the horrors that exist on the earth
> Arise from the evil minds of beings.
> Thus, if we can conquer the craziness of our minds,
> We will have conquered all of cyclic existence.

In this and previous lives, we've done many actions — some positive and some negative — and these imprints remain on our mindstreams. Dreading the unfortunate rebirth those imprints could bring, we'll seek help to prevent it. Having confidence that the Three Jewels can guide us to happiness leads us to seek refuge in them.


# Taking Refuge

Taking refuge is entrusting ourselves to the guidance of the Three Jewels — the Buddhas, Dharma and Sangha. By knowing the qualities of the Three Jewels and their ability to guide us from the danger of unfortunate rebirths and show us the path to happiness, we'll trust their instructions.

Buddhas are those beings who have completely removed all disturbing attitudes, karma and obscurations from their mindstreams.

They also have fully developed their good qualities. Thus, Buddhas have the compassion, wisdom and skillful means to indicate to us the path to happiness that they themselves followed.

Those beings who are now Buddhas haven't always been enlightened. They were once caught in the net of cyclic existence, plagued by their attachment, anger and ignorance, just as we are. However, by practicing the path, they purified their minds and developed their qualities, thus attaining enlightenment, the state of perfection. We can do the same if we follow the instructions they gave from their own experience.

Shakyamuni Buddha is often referred to as "the Buddha." He lived 2,500 years ago, and is the Buddha of this historical period. However, there are many Buddhas, and we can turn to all of them for refuge. Some Buddhas reside in pure lands, those places created by the power of their positive potential and enlightening influence. Buddhas can also manifest as beings in our world in whatever forms are suitable to guide us. They don't identify themselves, but instead appear as ordinary beings. Through their behavior or their teachings they guide us on the path.

The Buddhas are fully qualified guides because they have completely gone beyond cyclic existence. Therefore, their wisdom, compassion and skill in helping others aren't limited. Worldly deities, such as those born as gods, are still subject to death and rebirth under the influence of disturbing attitudes and karma, and thus aren't able to guide us to liberation.

In addition, Buddhas have skillful means by which they lead us. There are numerous stories in the Buddhist scriptures (sutras), of extremely ignorant, angry or greedy people whom the Buddha was able to lead to liberation.

Buddhas have great compassion and thus definitely will help us. In addition, they are impartial, and thus guide us no matter how we treat them in return. Buddhas don't play favorites like ordinary beings. Nor are they offended by others' criticism and flattered by their praise.

The Buddhas' help extends to all beings equally, just as the rays of the sun radiate in all directions. However, sunshine can't enter a covered pot. Similarly, the Buddhas' enlightening influence can't reach the minds of beings with many obscurations and little positive potential. If the pot is later uncovered, the sun's rays enter easily. Thus, it's important for us to eliminate our obscurations and make our minds as receptive to the Buddhas' influence as we can.

The Dharma refuge is the last two of the Four Noble Truths: true cessation and true path. That is, Dharma is the realizations of the path and absence of suffering and its causes on the mindstreams of those who have directly realized emptiness. In a more general sense, Dharma refers to the Buddha's teachings.

It's said that the Dharma is the real refuge. This means the realizations (clear understandings) and cessations (stopping of suffering and its causes) that we gain are our real protection. The Buddhas show us the way; the Sangha provide an example and help us to practice. But our own realizations will directly stop our pain and confusion.

The Sangha refuge refers to those persons — ordained or lay — who have direct perception of emptiness. These include arhats, as well as the hearers, solitary realizers and bodhisattvas who have realized emptiness directly. Because they perceive reality as it is, they can help us do the same.

In a more general sense, Sangha refers to the communities of monks and nuns who have dedicated their lives to practicing the path, although the individuals themselves may or may not have realizations. Individual monks and nuns are following the path, but it's not correct for us to expect them to be perfect beings yet.

Buddhist deities such as Avalokiteshvara (Kuan Yin, Chenresig), Manjushri and others may be regarded as Buddhas or as bodhisattva Sangha. We can view them in a variety of ways. In one way, they are historical beings, and we can read their biographies in the sutras. Regarding them in this way, we're inspired by the examples of their lives, and are encouraged to practice as they did.

Another way to regard these deities is as manifestations of magnificent qualities. Thus it's said that Avalokiteshvara is the manifestation of compassion, and Manjushri is the emanation of the wisdom of all the Buddhas. Both Avalokiteshvara and Manjushri have the same realizations, for the omniscient minds of all Buddhas have the same qualities and know the same things. However, in this case, Avalokiteshvara and Manjushri are seen as symbols of specific qualities.

Sometimes it's difficult for us to conceive of great compassion for all beings. But when this quality is symbolically and artistically represented, we can understand it better. With many arms outstretched to help others and many eyes to see their needs, the physical appearance of Avalokiteshvara reminds us of compassion. Thus we meditate on Avalokiteshvara to develop all enlightened realizations, especially compassion.

Once someone has become a Buddha, he or she (in actual fact a Buddha has no sex) may appear in the form of any of the deities. Thus, the omniscient mind of one Buddha can simultaneously appear in the form of Avalokiteshvara to benefit some people, in the form of Manjushri to benefit others, as our Dharma teacher, as an animal or even as an inanimate object like a bridge. Once someone's mindstream is fully purified and developed, it has the ability to appear in a wide variety of forms to benefit others and lead them to enlightenment.

We may view the deities in yet a third way: as our own Buddha potential in its future, fully developed form. In this way, when we turn to the Buddha for guidance, we remind ourselves that the Buddha we'll become is the one who ultimately will protect us from suffering. This encourages us to remember and develop the Buddha potential existing within ourselves right now.

An analogy illustrates how to relate to the Three Jewels. We are like a sick person, afflicted by sufferings and their causes. The Buddha is the doctor who diagnoses and prescribes medicine. The Dharma is the medicine, and the Sangha are the nurses who help us take it. In this way, we'll be cured and will be well and happy.

# Karma: the Law of Cause and Effect

The first medicine the Buddha prescribed for us is to observe karma, i.e. we have to abandon destructive actions and act positively. Thus, he explained the ten destructive actions, which were described in the previous chapter. Karma was also discussed in the chapter "Mind is the Creator of Our Experience." There are four principal characteristics of karma:

1. Karma is definite. When we plant apple seeds, apples grow, not

oranges. Similarly, when we act positively, happiness follows, never suffering. When we act destructively, misery comes, never happiness.

2. Karma is expandable. Just as a small seed can grow into a huge tree with much fruit, small actions can bring large results. Therefore, we should try to avoid even small negative actions and to create small positive ones.

3. If the cause isn't created, the result doesn't occur. If no seed is planted, nothing grows. The person who hasn't created the cause to be killed, won't be even if she is in a car crash.

Likewise, if we don't create the cause to realize the path, we won't realize it. Mere praying to the Buddha won't bring the effect we wish if we do nothing to create the principal cause. People who pray for wealth and yet are miserly are like those who pray to pass their exams but don't study. We must create the appropriate causes for something to occur. Prayer then stimulates the cause to mature.

4. Karma doesn't get lost. If we act positively, the happy result will eventually occur. When we do negative actions, the imprints aren't lost even though they may not bring their results immediately.

Through study and contemplation, we can gain a clear understanding of the functioning of karma. Although we can't go beyond the bounds of cause and effect, there is flexibility within it. Karma isn't cast in concrete and can be changed. For example, if we get angry or have wrong views, we impede our positive karma from ripening. If we purify negative imprints from our minds, we can impede or completely prevent them from maturing.

Thus, it's wise for us to engage in the four opponent powers to purify negative karma:

1. Regret our destructive actions. With wisdom, we recognize and admit our errors. Regret is different from guilt, for the latter immobilizes us emotionally and is based on misconception. Regret, on the other hand, comes from an honest assessment of our actions and enables us to learn from our mistakes.

2. Take refuge and generate the altruistic intention. When we have acted destructively in relation to either holy beings or ordinary beings, by taking refuge in the Three Jewels we restore our relationship with the holy beings; and by generating love, compassion and altruism, we restore our relationship with ordinary beings.

3. Determine not to do those negative actions in the future. The stronger our determination, the easier it will be to avoid habitually acting destructively.

4. Engage in a remedial practice. In general, this could be any virtuous action: helping those in need; offering service to our community; listening, reflecting or meditating on the Dharma; bowing or making offerings to the Three Jewels; printing Dharma books, etc.

   This concludes the initial step. It describes the practice of someone who seeks good future rebirths: taking refuge in the Three Jewels and observing the law of cause and effect by avoiding destructive actions and creating constructive ones.

# THE SECOND STEP:

*The wish for freedom*

Initial practitioners prepare to be able to die peacefully and to have a happy rebirth. Although this may appear to be future-oriented and to ignore happiness in the present, in fact the opposite is true. By being concerned with future lives, we'll be more aware of what is happening in the present, because our present actions create our future experiences.

Also, to avoid harmful actions, we'll endeavor to subdue the attachment, anger, closed-mindedness etc. that cause them. If we do this, our minds will be freer to live in the present without the worries, anxieties and distractions caused by disturbing attitudes. Paradoxically, concern for future lives leads us to live more in the present.

After a while, we may begin to think, "Even though my rebirths will be fortunate, still I'm caught in cyclic existence. Is this a satisfactory situation?"

Good rebirths are temporary measures to prevent the suffering of unfortunate ones. But we're still subjected to birth, sickness, aging and death without choice. There is no lasting security in any rebirth, for each of them, even the most wonderful ones, comes to an end. Controlled by disturbing attitudes, we go up and down, from one rebirth with its problems to the next with new problems.

Understanding this, a determination will grow within us to be free from all rebirths. Wishing to leave cyclic existence behind, we'll aspire for liberation, a state of lasting peace founded on wisdom. To attain this, we need to strive to develop the concentrated wisdom that can cut the root ignorance.

The four noble truths and noble eightfold path are generally discussed under the middle level. As these have been discussed previously, only a summary of the middle level is presented here. However, the four noble truths and noble eightfold path aren't restricted to the intermediate scope. For example, right action, speech and livelihood are the basic practice of a person on the initial level.

Contemplating the four noble truths leads us to generate the determination to be free from cyclic existence. The three higher trainings are the essential practice leading to liberation.

# THE THIRD STEP:

*Seeking enlightenment for the benefit of all*

At the initial level of spiritual practice, people prepare for death and future lives. This makes sense to them, and they're capable of doing this. After a while, when their understanding increases, they realize that good rebirths alone won't bring lasting happiness. Their goals expand, and they want to be completely free from the cycle of uncontrolled rebirth. They now become practitioners of the intermediate level and seek liberation.

Later, they may again reassess their goals, and ask, "Is my own attainment of liberation sufficient? What about everyone else?" They now develop a strong sense of universal responsibility for the welfare of all others. Thus they develop the bodhicitta: the altruistic intention to attain enlightenment to benefit all beings.

The Buddha taught two methods to cultivate the altruistic intention. One is the seven points of cause and result, which was emphasized by the sages Maitreya and Asanga. The other is exchanging self and others. This was elaborated upon by the Indian master Shantideva. For the sake of brevity, only the seven points of cause and effect will be discussed here.

Before cultivating the seven points of cause and effect, it's necessary to develop equanimity, an equal feeling towards all beings, which is free from attachment to our friends, aversion to enemies and apathetic indifference towards strangers. (Here "enemy" means anyone with whom we don't get along or who makes us uneasy.)

As long as we rigidly discriminate people as friends, enemies and strangers, it's impossible for us to develop impartial love for each of them. Therefore equanimity not only pacifies confused emotions towards others, but also is the basis for cultivating genuine love and compassion for them.

Attachment, aversion and indifference towards others arises when we only regard their immediate, superficial characteristics. For example, today Sue gives us a present and Joe gossips about us, so we consider Sue our friend and Joe our enemy. Tomorrow Joe gives us a gift and Sue talks behind our back. Suddenly our feelings change, and Joe is a friend and Sue is an enemy.

In fact, both Sue and Joe have acted similarly, so how can we say one is a real friend and the other a real enemy? If we look beyond their superficial actions, we would see that both have good qualities and both have weaknesses. Thus having attachment to one because he or she is "good" and aversion for the other who is "bad," is an unrealistic response.

In addition, our relationships with them as friend, enemy or stranger are temporary. When we were born, Sue and Joe were strangers and we were indifferent to them. Sue then became our friend and later our enemy, while for Joe it was the opposite. These relationships are likely to change again, with Sue becoming a friend or a stranger, and Joe becoming our enemy again or even a stranger.

Throughout our previous lives, everyone has been been a friend, enemy and stranger at some time. Our relationships with others are in constant flux. Therefore, attachment, aversion and indifference to them are inappropriate. The Buddha said:

> Those who at present hold a hostile attitude towards us have been our beloved mother, father, friend, brother and sister countless times. Those who benefit us now have also been our bitter enemy. Therefore, we should cast away resentment towards those who harm us, cast away attachment to those we like, and thus extend a loving mind towards all beings equally.

Recognizing that no person is our inherent, ever-lasting friend, enemy or stranger releases us from the confused emotions of attachment, aversion and indifference. This in turn will create in us an equal feeling of openness and concern for each person. We'll no longer feel alienated from some people or fearful that others will desert us.

From the basis of equanimity, we can proceed to develop the altruistic intention through the seven points of cause and effect. There are six causes:

1.  recognizing that all beings have been our mother
2.  remembering our mothers' kindness towards us
3.  wishing to repay that kindness
4.  love

5. compassion
6. great determination.

These six result in the seventh point, the altruistic intention, or bodhicitta.

# 1. Recognizing That All Beings Have Been Our Mother

The first step is to recognize that all beings have been our mother. In this meditation, our mother is chosen because in general, people feel close to their mothers. However, if we have a difficult relationship with our mother, we may choose our father, grandparents or whoever was very kind to us when we were young.

Recognizing that the countless number of beings have all been our mother challenges us to go beyond the confines of our present way of thinking. First, we must have some feeling that rebirth exists: that who we are now is one in a series of lives without beginning.

Because it may seem difficult to recognize that we haven't always been who we are now, it's helpful to think of the changes that occur in one lifetime. Imagine how differently we felt as infants: our bodies were different, our perception of the world was different. It almost feels as if those infants were different people, unrelated to the capable adults we are now.

If we envision ourselves as 90 years old, it seems as if those forgetful and bent-over old people are unrelated to us. However, the infants, our present selves and the old people exist in one continuity. We can be all of them.

Similarly, our minds can exist in a variety of other bodies. We've had many previous lives. Thus, we've had many mothers who have given birth to us and raised us during those lives. Our present mother hasn't always been our mother, for in previous lives we may have been born in one place and she in another. Thus, many beings have been our mothers in previous lives.

Since we have had an infinite number of previous lives, all beings at one time or another have been our mother. Because our minds are obscured by ignorance, we can't remember their having been our mother, and because we have taken new bodies, we don't recognize them in this life. However, if we remind ourselves that all beings have been our mothers, then whenever we see someone, there will be a spontaneous feeling of closeness.

For example, let's say when we were young, we were accidentally separated from our parents, whom we loved very much. Thirty years later, we walk down the street and see two beggars. At first we ignore them or are even hostile towards them. Then we look again, and suddenly we realize they are our parents. They look different and so do we, so at first we don't recognize each other. But when we do, we suddenly feel an extraordinary concern and love for those beggars. We have no reservation about helping them. It's similar with training ourselves to recognize that all beings have been our parents in previous lives.

## 2. Remembering our Mothers' Kindness towards Us

The second step is to remember the kindness others have shown us as our mothers. To do this, we initially take the example of our present mother or whoever cared for us when we were young. Our mother carried us in her womb for nine months, even though pregnancy was very uncomfortable. She happily endured the pain of giving birth to us, cared for us when we were helpless infants, putting up with  our childish temper tantrums and bad behavior. Although our mother probably didn't like to discipline us, she had to in order to teach us ethics and manners, thus enabling us to get along with others. She taught us to speak and made sure we had a good education. Within their financial limits, our parents bought us toys and took us on trips.

Some people find it uncomfortable to think about the kindness of their parents. They may feel that since they didn't ask to be born, they don't owe their parents anything. Some people resent their parents because their parents disciplined them severely, denied them things that other children had or even abused them.

If we feel this way, then we should reflect on the kindness of whomever helped us when we were young. Later, we may wish to learn the techniques the Buddha taught for reducing anger and developing patience and apply these to our relationship with our parents. It's important to remember that however dysfunctional our relationship with our parents may have been, they did make our precious human life possible. Whatever their motives were, they cared for us to the extent that they were physically and mentally capable. If we can appreciate this and forgive them for their weaknesses, our hearts will open towards them.

The purpose of remembering our mother's kindness isn't to generate attachment for her, because attachment is a disturbing attitude. Rather, we want to honestly recognize her kindness as this enables deep gratitude to arise in our minds. We then generalize this heart-warming gratitude to all beings by remembering they all have been our mothers in the past and have been as kind to us as our present mothers. This gratitude will lead us to the third step, wishing to repay their kindness.

## 3. Wishing to Repay that Kindness

When we recognize others' kindness, automatically we want to help them in return. This isn't a feeling of burdensome obligation towards them, but rather a spontaneous joy and concern for others.

## 4. Love

From this wish to repay their kindness, we'll go on to think how wonderful it would be if all those kind people could have happiness. This is love — the wish for them to be happy and to have the causes of happiness. Since we have previously freed ourselves from attachment to friends, aversion to enemies and apathetic indifference to strangers, our love will be impartial and will extend to everyone equally. We'll love others simply because they exist, with no strings attached. The Tibetan sage Lama Tzong Khapa said:

> From our point of view, all beings are equal to us because they have all been our beloved mothers, fathers, brothers, sisters and

friends countless times. From their point of view, all beings should also be treated as equal to us because they equally desire happiness and shun unhappiness. Therefore, we should try to maintain a loving mind towards all beings equally.

## 5. Compassion

When we consider the problems and pain that others undergo, we'll then generate compassion — the wish for others to be freed from all suffering and causes. Compassion is different from pity and other condescending attitudes. Compassion recognizes ourselves and others as equal in terms of wanting happiness and wanting to be free from misery, and enables us to help them with as much ease as we now help ourselves.

## 6. The Great Determination

Having deep compassion, we progress to the sixth step, assuming the responsibility to bring others happiness and to free them from suffering. Whereas previously we wanted others to be happy and to be free from misery, now we're making the great determination to do something about it.

## 7. The Altruistic Intention of Bodhicitta

But how can we lead others to happiness when we're confused ourselves? One drowning person can't save another; similarly one person caught in the web of cyclic existence can't show another the way out. To guide others, we must know their karmic predispositions, their inclinations and interests. We also must know all the teachings in order to teach others what is suitable for them.

Thus, to actualize our wish to lead others from suffering and to happiness, we need to have perfect compassion, wisdom and skillful means. As only a Buddha has these qualities, we must attain enlightenment to benefit others in the most effective way. This aspiration for enlightenment is the altruistic intention (bodhicitta). When we've become so familiar with this attitude that it is our spontaneous reaction to all others, then we'll become bodhisattvas, the spiritual children of the Buddhas. Because of this noble and magnificent attitude, our ability to help others will increase tremendously.

# THE FAR-REACHING ATTITUDES:

*Active compassion*

After generating the altruistic intention, the next step is to practice the six far-reaching attitudes which lead to enlightenment. Sometimes called the six perfections or six *paramitas*, they are generosity, ethics, patience, joyous effort, meditative stabilization and wisdom.

Practicing generosity, ethics and patience with joyous effort directly benefits others now. But the final aim of all six far-reaching attitudes is to actualize the wisdom directly perceiving emptiness. Through this wisdom, we'll then eliminate all disturbing attitudes and remove all stains and obscurations from our mindstreams, thus becoming fully enlightened Buddhas. At this point, our ability to help others will be totally developed.

Although these six are practiced throughout the path, at this point they're called far-reaching attitudes because they lead to the development of full wisdom, thus enabling us to reach far beyond cyclic existence. It's important for us to engage in the six far-reaching attitudes with an altruistic motivation, contemplate emptiness while we're practicing them, and dedicate the positive potential created to the enlightenment of all beings.

## Generosity

The first far-reaching attitude, generosity, is the willingness to give whatever we have to help others. This practice counteracts the miserliness and laziness that often arise when others approach us for help. There are three types of generosity:

1. giving material possessions,
2. protecting others who are suffering or in danger,
3. counseling others and teaching them the Dharma.

Most of us ordinary beings tend to be miserly and more concerned with protecting our own property than with making others happy by being generous. Often we fear that by giving something, we'll suffer from not having it. We give only as much as we have to in order not to lose face. Generally, we keep the best for ourselves and give whatever is left to others. After giving, we remind others how much we've done so they'll feel obliged to help us in return.

These miserly motivations create tension in our minds and prevent us from creating positive potential and gaining spiritual realizations. Miserliness is a selfish state of mind that considers our own happiness more important than others'. As long as we're miserly, we're never satisfied no matter how much we have.

When miserliness makes us hesitant to give, we should remember that our wealth is impermanent and one day we'll have to be separated from it. There's no sense in clinging to it. If we use it by sharing it with others, we'll counteract the miserliness that causes unfortunate rebirths. If we train ourselves to feel joy in giving, our generosity will bring happiness to others and to ourselves.

Generosity isn't a matter of guiltily telling ourselves we "should" give. It's developing a heart that finds genuine joy in making others happy. This doesn't mean we should give everything away so we have nothing and become a burden to those around us. Rather, we give according to our means. The amount isn't as important as the motivation.

It's crucial to give wisely. Offering an alcoholic a drink isn't charity; giving money for the purchase of weapons, poison and illegal drugs doesn't benefit anyone. We shouldn't harm some beings in order to give to others. Thus, it's not wise to kill animals or ask others to kill them so our family can have a nice meal.

It's best if we help people who are helpless, desperate, poor or sick. Also, by making offerings to sincere Dharma practitioners we supply them with the daily necessities to continue their practice. With our offerings to the Three Jewels, we support Dharma activities, construction of temples and facilities, publication of books and social services provided by temples.

The second type of generosity, giving protection, involves helping those who are suffering or in danger. This could include saving a drowning child, helping sick or old people who are neglected, working to prevent cruelty to animals, constructing hospices for the dying, and helping those with AIDS or cancer to receive proper medical attention. When there are earthquakes, floods and other natural disasters, we should help in whatever way we can.

Giving guidance and teachings, the third type of generosity, includes many activities. We can console those who are grieving or in difficulty. It's also beneficial to encourage others not to lie or cheat, and to act in constructive ways. By doing so, we show others the way to have more peace of mind now and to create the cause for future happiness. Chanting prayers so the sick or dying hear them and turn their minds toward virtuous thoughts is also beneficial.

The best gift to give others is the Dharma — instructing others on the path to enlightenment. This gives others the means to release themselves from all suffering and to attain lasting happiness.

## Ethics

The far-reaching attitude of ethics is safeguarding our body, speech and mind from negative actions. Ethics is extremely important, for without it we can't attain higher realizations.

Not understanding this, some people chant or meditate, but are careless about their behavior in daily life. They seem very holy when they're performing rites and rituals, but afterwards they take intoxicants, gossip and engage in shady business deals. Wanting to keep one foot in cyclic existence and the other in nirvana, these people don't progress on the path. The great Indian scholar and practitioner Atisha said:

> Most of us think that the practice of Dharma is to recite some commitment, visualize a deity, or chant. But real Dharma practice is the integration of positive activities into our lives. If we are aware of this, we might gain more realizations in our daily lives than during our sitting meditations.

The far-reaching attitude of ethics is of three types:

1. abandoning destructive actions,

2. carrying out constructive ones,
3. leading others to live ethically.

By abandoning the ten destructive actions and keeping whatever precepts we've taken, we'll free ourselves from the gross disturbing attitudes that propel us to act negatively. Thus, our minds automatically become calmer, less distracted and free from regret. This enables us to concentrate better during meditation.

By acting constructively, we'll enrich our minds with positive potential and will benefit others. By our example and by our instructions, we can then lead others to act ethically.

# Patience

Patience is inner calm and strength that enables us to act clearly in any difficult situation. There are three types of patience:

1. not being upset with those who harm us,
2. transcending problems and pain with a positive attitude,
3. enduring difficulties encountered in Dharma practice.

The first type of patience enables us to be clear-minded and calm no matter how others treat us. At present, when we receive harm, we often blame the other person and become agitated. Sometimes our agitation takes the form of self-pity and depression, and we complain about how badly others treat us. Other times, it becomes anger and we retaliate by harming the other person.

Patience acts as an antidote to this because it views the situation from a different perspective. As long as we're in cyclic existence, we're sure to meet people who cause us problems. This is the nature of our existence. But patience helps us have a broad perspective of the situation: because we acted negatively in the past, now we experience the consequences.

Thus, rather than see the other person as the principal cause of our pain, we'll recognize that our own disturbing attitudes and negative actions are the real source. Instead of harming other people, we'll put more energy into overcoming our disturbing attitudes and purifying our negative actions.

When people harm us, they're generally doing so because they're unhappy. If we truly understand this, we can stop being preoccupied with our own situation and consider the unhappiness of those who harm us. We know what it's like to be miserable, and that's how they're feeling. Thinking in this way, we can transform those who harm us into objects of our compassion.

We know that sometimes our disturbing attitudes take control of us, causing us to do and say harmful things. Similarly, people who harm us are under the influence of their own anger and jealousy. Just as we want people to forgive our shortcomings, so too do others wish us to be tolerant, and not take what they say and do to heart when their emotions get out of control.

Being patient doesn't mean being passive or cowardly and thus letting others do whatever they want. Rather, we should first free our own minds from anger and then look at the situation clearly. We can then try to do whatever is most beneficial for everyone in the situation, which may involve being firm and preventing someone from harming others.

The patience to transcend problems enables us to transform painful situations, such as sickness and poverty, into supports for our Dharma practice. Rather than becoming depressed or angry when we're plagued with difficulties, we'll learn from these experiences and face them with courage. Experiencing difficulties makes us more compassionate toward those in similar situations. Our pride is deflated, our understanding of cause and effect increases, and we won't be lazy to help someone in need.

Patience is a necessary quality when practicing Dharma, and developing this is the third type of patience. Sometimes it's difficult to understand the teachings, to control our minds, or to discipline ourselves to meditate daily. Patience helps us overcome this and to wrestle with our unruly minds. Rather than expecting instant results from practicing briefly, we'll have the patience to cultivate our minds continuously, over years.

# Joyous Effort

Joyous effort is essential if we are to make continual progress in Dharma. If we lack enthusiasm many hindrances arise, chiefly in the form of laziness. Laziness is of three kinds:

1. If we're attached to sleep and relaxation, we procrastinate and never get around to practicing;
2. If we're attached to worldly activities, we're too busy to study, contemplate and meditate;
3. Discouraged, we forsake our practice.

Joyous effort is the antidote to these three types of laziness. For instance, by remembering the transience of our lives and the certainty of death, our overindulgence in sleep will vanish. The preciousness of our human life will become clearer, and we'll want to use it wisely before we die.

Of course we have to sleep to be healthy, but too much sleep makes our minds dull and wastes our time. When we die, we'll have nothing to show for all the extra hours we spent lying around. However, if we use our time wisely to practice, our deaths will be peaceful and we'll have many good qualities and virtuous imprints to carry with us to future lives. As Shantideva said:

> Relying upon the boat of a human (body),
> Free yourself from the great river of pain (cyclic existence)
> As it is hard to find this boat again,
> This is no time for sleep, you fool!

From a Buddhist perspective, busying ourselves with worldly activities is a form of laziness, because we're lax in self-cultivation. Our lives are so busy in modern society: our appointment books are completely full and we're always running here and there. We often complain there isn't enough time for the Dharma.

However, whenever we have a spare moment we work overtime or call some friends to fill in the gap. We always have time to eat, but we hardly ever have time to nourish ourselves spiritually by attending

Dharma classes or meditating. When the temple has entertainment and free meals, we go; but when there is meditation or lessons, we're busy.

This hindrance to spiritual progress exists because we're attached to worldly pleasures: food, money, reputation, amusement, friends. The harm comes from our inappropriate way of relating to them. Attached, we selfishly indulge in them. These things in and of themselves aren't bad, however. By pacifying our disturbing attitudes, we can enjoy these things with a good motivation — to improve ourselves for the benefit of others.

By remembering the truth of suffering, we'll realize there's no lasting joy to be found in worldly pleasures. Enjoying them is like drinking salt water: rather than satisfying us, they make us crave for more. Similarly, no matter how much money we have, we never have enough; no matter how many times we go out drinking and to the movies, we still are dissatisfied; no matter how high we are on the corporate ladder, there's always someone who is higher.

Being attached to these things only keeps us ensnared in dissatisfaction in this life, and in constantly recurring problems in future lives. By reminding ourselves of this, we'll practice the Dharma enthusiastically and won't get side-tracked by senseless activities. As Lama Tzong Khapa said:

> There is no satisfaction in enjoying worldly pleasures. They are the door to all misery. Having realized that the fault of cyclic existence's perfections is that they cannot be trusted, may I be strongly intent on the bliss of liberation — inspire me thus!

This doesn't mean we become Dharma fanatics and refuse to talk with others or do our work. That is another extreme. What we should seek is a balance whereby we cultivate a good motivation for all activities we do, and leave aside useless activities that waste our time and lead us to act negatively.

The third type of laziness is discouragement: we may think that we're incompetent, that the bodhisattva path is too difficult, or that the goal of enlightenment is beyond our reach. This way of thinking makes our minds spiral downward into depression. Feeling hopeless, we abandon our efforts at practice.

It's important to remember we always have within us the Buddha nature — the potential within us to become fully enlightened Buddhas. This potential is our birthright and can never be taken away. If we follow the path — eliminating our obscurations and developing our good qualities — then Buddhahood is assured. Shantideva paraphrased the *The Questions of Subahu Sutra*:

> The *tathagatas* (Buddhas) who speak what is true
> Have uttered this truth:
>
> "If they develop the strength of their exertion,
> Even those who are flies, mosquitoes, bees and insects
> Will win the unsurpassable enlightenment
> Which is so hard to find."
>
> So, if I do not forsake the bodhisattvas' way of life,
> Why should someone like myself who has been born in the
>     human race
> Not attain enlightenment, since I am able to recognize
> What is beneficial and what is of harm?

## Meditative Stabilization

Many of the important points about meditative stabilization were discussed under the higher training in concentration. As was noted, non-Buddhists also develop concentration and can gain clairvoyant powers due to their practice. However, when Buddhists practice meditative stabilization, it's supported by refuge in the Three Jewels and the determination to be free from cyclic existence. Thus, when Buddhists join together the meditative stabilizations of calm abiding and penetrative insight into emptiness, they will attain liberation. In addition, when they develop the altruistic aspiration for enlightenment, their meditative stabilization will lead to full enlightenment or Buddhahood.

Because the motivation with which we engage in meditation determines the result of our practice, it's important to take refuge in the Three Jewels and develop a virtuous aspiration at the beginning of every meditation session. To help us do this, we can recite the following prayers:

> I take refuge in the Buddhas,
> I take refuge in the Dharma,
> I take refuge in the Sangha.

> I take refuge until I am enlightened in the Buddhas, the Dharma and the Sangha. By the positive potential I create by practicing generosity and the other far-reaching attitudes, may I attain Buddhahood in order to benefit all beings.

> May all beings have happiness and its causes,
> May all beings be free from suffering and its causes,
> May all beings not be separated from sorrowless bliss,
> May all beings abide in equanimity, free from bias, attachment and anger.

These prayers help to prepare our minds for meditation. Having generated a good motivation at the beginning, we'll have less distraction during the actual meditation session. Our meditation object could be the breath, the four mindfulnesses, love and compassion, visualization and recitation of mantra, or analytic meditation in which we think about a subject the Buddha taught.

At the conclusion of the session, we should dedicate the positive potential created during our meditation for the benefit of all beings. Sometimes people call this dedication "transference of merits." This doesn't mean our positive potential is transferred to another person's consciousness like money is transferred from one bank to another, for this would contradict the law of cause and effect. When we create positive potential and dedicate it to others' well-being, it acts as a cooperative condition, enabling their own good karmic imprints to mature.

Dedication safeguards our positive potential from being destroyed if we later become angry or have wrong views. It also prevents us from being attached to our own spiritual achievements. We can dedicate as follows:

Due to this positive potential, may I soon attain the enlightened state of a Buddha, so that I may be able to liberate all beings from their sufferings.

# Wisdom

The far-reaching attitude of wisdom is of three types:

1. wisdom understanding that emptiness of inherent existence is the ultimate nature of all phenomena,
2. conventional intelligence knowing grammar, logic, science, the arts and so forth,
3. wisdom knowing how to benefit others.

The first wisdom is the key to liberation and enlightenment. Emptiness is a profound subject, and it's best to study with a qualified master to understand it fully. What follows is only an introduction to the subject.

There are many advantages to developing the wisdom realizing emptiness. This specific type of wisdom is the sole means to eliminate our ignorance and other disturbing attitudes. It is also the most powerful tool for purifying negative karmic imprints. In addition, it enables us to benefit others effectively, for we can then teach them how to gain this wisdom themselves.

Our ignorance prevents us from perceiving how we and other phenomena exist. It also misconceives how things exist, projecting a false way of existence onto them. By realizing that things are free from the fantasized projections we put on them, we prevent disturbing attitudes from arising. An example will make this clear.

We can become very emotional about money. If we see a large amount, we often become excited and start to think of everything we could buy if that money were ours. If we lose our money, we're worried and upset, for something of value is gone.

It appears to us that the money has an inherent worth: in and of itself it's important. It seems the money and its value exist inside those bills, independent of anything else. We need only look at our reaction if someone burns a large bill to see that we spontaneously feel the money is inherently valuable.

Let's look again. What is money? It's paper with ink designs on it. That's all. On the basis of paper printed with certain designs, we add value and importance. In and of itself, the paper is worthless. Only because we assign the label "money" to those pieces of paper do they become currency. Only because as a society we give value to this currency does it have worth.

The money, as well as its value, exist because our minds attribute names and meaning to those printed pieces of paper. That is, the money exists due to the power of our concepts about those pieces of paper. In actual fact, the money is empty of inherent or independent existence. This is because it exists dependently: it depends on its causes (for example, the trees from which the paper came), its parts (front, back, right, left), and our minds that labeled it "money" and attached value to it.

Why is it important to understand that money is empty of inherent existence and yet exists dependently? Because this awareness will prevent us from overestimating its importance. If we don't understand emptiness, then we could develop many disturbing ideas and reactions to money. For example, some people are obsessed by it, remaining dissatisfied no matter how much they have; some become proud and flaunt their wealth; others quarrel and even injure people to get money.

If we understand that money is a creation of our society, dependent upon our conceptual minds as well as upon the printed paper, then we'll have more realistic attitudes towards it.

Similarly, all phenomena and persons exist by depending on other factors: prior causes and conditions, their constituent parts, and the conceptual minds that label them. This is the meaning of "dependent arising." Thus, emptiness and dependent arising complement each other. Things are empty because they depend on other factors. Things exist conventionally because they are empty of an independent nature.

People and phenomena don't have inherent or independent existence, nor are they totally non-existent. The meaning of emptiness and dependent arising falls between these two extremes: this is the view of the middle way taught by the Buddha. Lama Tzong Khapa said in *The Three Principles of the Path*:

In addition, appearances clear away the extreme of (inherent) existence; emptiness clears away the extreme of non-existence. When you understand the arising of cause and effect from the viewpoint of emptiness, you are not captivated by either of the extreme views.

The first step toward the realization of emptiness is listening to teachings and studying books on the subject. Then we should think about what we've learned and discuss it with others to eliminate our wrong ideas. Third, we need to meditate, integrating what we've understood with our mindstreams.

Two elements are important in the meditation on emptiness. The first is calm abiding (*samatha*), the ability to keep our mind single-pointedly on the meditation object, in this case emptiness. The second is special insight (*vipassana*), the wisdom factor which correctly analyzes and discerns emptiness. Actual special insight is combined with calm abiding.

By repeatedly meditating on emptiness, we'll totally dispel all wrong conceptions and disturbing attitudes from our mindstreams. Because our meditation is motivated by the altruistic intention, it will result in enlightenment.

# PRACTICAL GUIDELINES FOR GOOD LIVING

Taking refuge in the Buddhas, Dharma and Sangha helps us to focus on what is important in our lives. It gives our lives a positive direction and reaffirms our conviction that there exists a path to happiness.

When taking refuge, we're enriched by the knowledge that great beings with full compassion, wisdom and skillful means exist. We gain confidence that by following the path, we'll attain the same state they have. Refuge is also a way of fulfilling a promise we've made to ourselves — a promise to become better people and make a positive contribution to others' welfare.

The real taking of refuge occurs deep in our hearts and isn't dependent on doing or saying anything. Nevertheless, we may wish to participate in the refuge ceremony by requesting a monk or nun to formally give us refuge. The refuge ceremony is brief: we repeat a passage after our teacher and open our hearts to make a strong connection with the Three Jewels of the Buddhas, Dharma and Sangha. The ceremony also "officially" makes us a Buddhist.

The reason we take refuge is to prevent future suffering and to progress along the path. To be true to our goals, we must act according to this motivation after taking refuge. It's not the case that after we take refuge we're "saved," and thereafter can do anything we please. Taking refuge is the first step in giving our lives a positive direction, and we must continue to channel our energy in that direction. Therefore, the Buddha gave advice on how to practice the Dharma to ensure we remain true to our determination to improve ourselves. The points to train ourselves in are:

1.    In keeping with taking refuge in the Buddha, we should rely on a qualified spiritual master. Whoever performs the refuge ceremony for us becomes one of our spiritual mentors. We may have more than one teacher, and it's good to pray to meet fully qualified mentors with whom we feel a close Dharma connection. It's beneficial if we follow

the Dharma instructions our teachers give us, care for our teachers' needs and treat them with respect.

2.    In keeping with taking refuge in the Dharma, we should listen to and study the teachings, as well as put them into practice in our daily lives. Some people think only monks and nuns study the teachings deeply, and such dedicated study and practice is too difficult for lay followers. This is incorrect. Everyone should listen to and study the teachings as much as possible. If we want to progress along the path, we must practice the Dharma, and receiving instructions is essential in order to practice.

3.    In keeping with taking refuge in the Sangha, we should respect the Sangha as our spiritual companions and follow their good example. If we constantly look for others' weaknesses, that's all we'll see. Such an attitude prevents us from appreciating whatever good qualities they have and learning from them.

We shouldn't expect monks and nuns to be perfect. Although they have dedicated their lives to the path, it takes time to gain realizations, and most of the Sangha are endeavoring to pacify their disturbing attitudes and karma, just as we are. Shaving one's head doesn't make one enlightened. However, we can appreciate their effort to practice the Dharma purely, and the good example they set for us. Although individual monks and nuns may have faults, we should respect the fact they have taken the vows set forth by the Buddha.

4.    We should try to train ourselves in accordance to the examples set by the Buddhas, Dharma and Sangha. If we take their behavior as a model, we'll eventually become like them. When we're in a state of emotional turmoil, it's helpful to ask ourselves, "How would a bodhisattva respond to this situation?" Thinking about this, we'll consider other ways to handle our problem.

5.    We should avoid being self-indulgent, running after any desirable object we see. Craving money and status leads us to obsession and constant dissatisfaction. We're much happier when we enjoy pleasures of the senses in moderation.

Similarly, let's avoid arrogantly criticizing whatever we dislike. It's so easy to see others' faults and overlook our own. Yet this doesn't make us or others any happier. It is more constructive to correct our own faults than to point out those of others.

6.     As much as possible we should avoid the ten destructive actions and keep precepts. We can take the five lay precepts for the duration of our lives, or the eight precepts for one day. Ethics is the foundation of the practice of the Dharma; without it, there is no way to create the cause for good rebirths or to attain realizations.

7.     We should develop a compassionate and sympathetic heart toward all other beings. To do this, it's helpful to continually meditate on love, compassion and altruism. If we don't contemplate patience before meeting a troublesome person, it will be difficult to control our temper. We need to prepare beforehand, by remembering the kindness of others and meditating on patience continually in our daily meditation sessions. Chapter six of Shantideva's *A Guide to the Bodhisattva's Way of Life* is very effective in helping us learn the antidotes to anger.

If we nurture patience in our meditation, then when we go to work or school, we'll be mindful and will notice when we're getting angry. At that time, we will be able to remember what we've contemplated in the meditation sessions and let go of our anger. We won't always succeed, but over time we'll notice progress.

Each evening it's helpful to review our day. If we discover any remaining anger in our minds, we should again reflect on patience and the altruistic intention.

8.     On Buddhist festival days, it's advisable for us to make special offerings to the Three Jewels to accumulate positive potential.

Points 5 - 7 emphasize the importance of improving our relations with others. Following Buddha's teachings doesn't mean performing rites and rituals to gain a superficial feeling of being "holy." It means not harming others and helping them as much as possible in our daily lives.

# Specific Guidelines

To help us develop and maintain a good relationship with each of the Three Jewels individually, there are guidelines which are specific for refuge in the Buddhas, Dharma and Sangha:

1. Having taken refuge in the Buddha, who has purified all defilements and developed all qualities, we shouldn't turn for refuge to worldly gods who lack the capacity to guide us from all problems. Although some worldly gods have psychic powers, they aren't free from cyclic existence. Taking ultimate refuge in them is like one drowning person asking another to take him to shore.

We should respect all images of the Buddha and avoid putting them in low or dirty places, stepping over them or pointing our feet toward them. Because the statues represent the noble state we want to attain, we should take care of them. The statues don't need our respect, but we need to be mindful of the Buddha's qualities that they represent.

The purpose of having statues of Buddha is to help us remember the enlightened state and work toward attaining it ourselves. Therefore we shouldn't use religious objects as collateral for a loan or buy and sell them as someone buys and sells used cars — with the motive to earn a living. The profit made from selling statues or Dharma books should be used to purchase or produce more Dharma items, not to buy ourselves a good meal or new clothes.

When looking at various images, it's nonsensical to discriminate, "This Buddha is beautiful, but this one isn't." How can a Buddha be ugly? We can comment on the artist's skills in making a statue or painting, but not on the looks of a Buddha.

Also, don't treat expensive statues with respect while neglecting those that are damaged or less costly. Some people put the expensive beautifully-made statues in the front of their shrines so their friends will say, "You have such lovely and costly things in your home!" Seeking praise for owning religious objects is a worldly attitude, and we might as well show off our VCR or bankbook if all we're looking for is admiration from others.

2.    Having taken refuge in the Dharma, we should avoid harming any living being. One becomes a Buddha in order to benefit others, and Buddhas cherish others more than themselves. Therefore, if we admire the Buddhas, we should respect all living beings just as they do.

Also, we should respect the written words which describe the path to enlightenment by keeping the texts clean and in a high place. Avoid stepping over them, putting them on the floor, or throwing them in the rubbish when they are old. Old Dharma materials can be burned.

The reason for this is not that the paper and ink of the books are holy in and of themselves, but that these books show the path to enlightenment which we want to develop in our minds. They are our spiritual nourishment. We don't put our food on the floor without something to contain it, because the floor is dirty and we value our food. Similarly, if we remember the importance of Dharma books which nourish us spiritually, we'll treat them properly. These guidelines make us more mindful of how we relate to things in our environment.

3.    Having taken refuge in the Sangha, we should avoid becoming close friends with people who criticize the Buddhas, Dharma and Sangha, or who are unruly or harm others. We avoid these people not because they're "evil and bad," but because our own minds are weak. For example, although we may want to stop gossiping, if we're constantly in the company of people who gossip, we'll easily resume our old habits.

However, we shouldn't criticize or be rude to these people. We can have compassion for them, but we won't seek their company. For example, if a colleague is critical of our religious practice, we can be courteous and kind to him at work, but we won't cultivate his friendship after work or discuss religion with him. However, if someone is open-minded and wants to discuss religion in order to understand life, we can freely engage ideas with him.

The bodhisattvas and practitioners approaching arhatship, who don't run the risk of falling back into their old negative behaviors, seek the company of unruly beings in order to help them. However, if our practice isn't yet firm, we have to be careful of the environment we put ourselves in.

Also, we should respect monks and nuns as people who earnestly endeavor to actualize the teachings. Respecting them helps our minds, because it opens us to appreciate their qualities and learn from their examples. By respecting even the robes of ordained beings, we'll be happy and inspired on seeing them.

## Common Guidelines

To help us deepen our refuge and extend it to others, there are six guidelines in common for the Three Jewels:

1.    Mindful of the qualities of the Three Jewels and the differences between them and other possible refuges, we should repeatedly take refuge in the Buddhas, Dharma and Sangha. The qualities of the Three Jewels are explained in many texts. If we study these, our understanding of how the Three Jewels guide and protect us will increase. Taking refuge isn't done just once. Rather, it's a process through which we continually deepen our trust in the Three Jewels.

2.    Remembering the kindness of the Three Jewels, we should make offerings to them. Some people make offerings thinking that they're paying the Three Jewels back for what they've done or are obliging them to render help in the future. These people go to the temple and pray, "Buddha, if you make my sick relative recover and make my business flourish, I'll make offerings to you each year on this day."

This is the wrong attitude to have when making offerings. We aren't doing business with the Buddha, as with the attitude, "Buddha, you deliver what I want, then I'll pay you." Offerings should be made with a good motivation, to eliminate our miserliness and to increase our joy in giving.

Some people make offerings as if they were in the business of earning merit. They regard merit as spiritual money and strive to collect it with a greedy mind. This is also an incorrect attitude. While it's beneficial to create positive potential, it's important to dedicate it for the welfare of everyone.

It's good to offer our food before eating. This enables us to stop and reflect for a moment, rather than gobble our food down with voracity the way hungry animals do. To offer our food, we think, "Food is like medicine which cures the suffering of hunger. I must preserve my life so that I can practice the Dharma and be of service to others. Food is the fuel which allows me to do so. Many beings were involved in growing, transporting and preparing this food. They were very kind, and to repay this I want to make my life meaningful. I can do this by offering the food to the Buddha with the motivation to become a Buddha myself for their benefit."

Then imagine the food as pure and sweet wisdom-nectar that gives great bliss. Visualize a small Buddha made of light at your heart center and offer this nectar to him or her. To consecrate it, recite "om ah hum" three times. This is a mantra representing the qualities of the Buddha's body, speech and mind. Then recite the following verses:

> I now take this food, without greed or repulsion,
> Nor merely for health, not for pleasure or comfort,
> But simply as a medicine to strengthen my body
> To attain enlightenment for the benefit of all.
>
> The supreme teacher, the precious Buddha,
> The supreme refuge, the holy precious Dharma,
> The supreme guide, the precious Sangha,
> To all of the objects of refuge I make this offering.
>
> May myself and all those around me
> Never be separated from the Three Jewels in all future lives,
> May we continuously make offerings to the Three Jewels,
> May we receive the blessings and inspiration of the Three Jewels.

While doing this, we can close our eyes for a few moments, or if we're in a public place, we can visualize and say the prayers silently, with our eyes open.

3.    Mindful of the compassion of the Three Jewels, we should

encourage others to take refuge in them. When we recall how the Buddhas practiced the path and how the Sangha is practicing the path to help us, their compassion towards us becomes obvious. Their kindness to teach us the Dharma, guide us, set a good example and inspire us is inconceivably vast.

Aware of the benefit that taking refuge and following the Dharma has had on our own lives, we'll want to share this fortune with others. However, pressuring people to come to Dharma talks or forcing our beliefs on others is both unskillful and rude. We shouldn't have a football team mentality thinking, "My religion is better than yours. I'm going to win more converts than you." We aren't in competition with other religions.

Nor should we go to the other extreme, keeping all Buddhist activities quiet, not publicizing them at all. If no one had organized and publicized Buddhist teachings, I never would have heard about the Dharma. I'm grateful to those who created the opportunity for me to contact and practice the Buddha's teachings.

Similarly, we can let others know about Buddhist teachings and activities and encourage them to come if they wish. To people who have no interest in Buddhism per se, we can express the meaning of the teachings in ordinary language. After all, much of Buddhism is common sense. For instance, we can talk to others about the faults of anger and how to calm hatred, without using any Buddhist vocabulary. We can explain the disadvantages of selfishness and the advantages of kindness toward others in ordinary language.

In addition, others will notice our behavior and will wonder how we're able to remain calm and happy in bad circumstances. We needn't speak one word of Dharma to them, but by our actions they'll see the benefits of Dharma practice and will be curious about what we do. Some of my relatives once said to me, "You didn't get angry when that person criticized you!" After that, they became more open to learning about Buddhism.

4.   Remembering the benefits of taking refuge, we should take refuge three times in the morning and three times in the evening, by reciting and reflecting upon any of the refuge prayers.

It's extremely beneficial to start our day off in a positive way.

When the alarm clock rings, let's try to make our first thoughts, "How fortunate I am to be alive and to have the opportunity to practice Dharma. The Three Jewels are reliable guides to lead me along the path to enlightenment. The best way to take the essence from my life is to develop the attitude of cherishing others and wanting to benefit them. Therefore, today, as much as possible, I'll avoid harming others and will be kind and help them."

Then we can recite three times the prayer for taking refuge and generating the altruistic intention:

I take refuge until I am enlightened in the Buddhas, the Dharma and the Sangha. By the positive potential I create by practicing generosity and the other far-reaching attitudes (ethics, patience, joyous effort, meditative stabilization and wisdom), may I attain Buddhahood in order to benefit all beings.

It takes only a few moments to think about these things and to recite the prayer, yet doing so has a significant effect on the rest of our day. We'll be more cheerful and will be sure of our direction in life. Especially if we don't do a regular meditation practice, starting the day in this way is extremely beneficial.

In the evening, after reviewing the day's activities and freeing our minds from any remaining disturbing attitudes that may have arisen during the day, we should again take refuge and generate the altruistic intention.

Before going to sleep, we can envision the Buddha, made of light, on our pillow. Placing our head in his lap, we'll fall asleep amidst the gentle glow of his wisdom and compassion.

5.    We should do all actions by entrusting ourselves to the Three Jewels. When we're nervous, it's good to visualize the Buddha, make requests, and imagine light radiating  from the Buddha which enters our body, filling it completely. If we're in danger, we can make prayers and request the Three Jewels for help and guidance.

Entrusting ourselves to the Three Jewels also refers to remembering their instructions. For example, when we become angry, we should recall the techniques to cultivate patience. When we feel jealous, we can instead rejoice in others' happiness and good qualities. Our Dharma practice is our best refuge, for with it we'll develop the beneficial and correct attitudes that resolve our problems.

6.     We shouldn't forsake our refuge if our lives are threatened or for a joke. Whether we're happy or sad, maintaining confidence in and a good relationship with the Three Jewels is important. Some people become so distracted when enjoying pleasures of the senses that they forget their Dharma practice. Others become so discouraged when misfortune strikes that they forget the Three Jewels. Forgetting our refuge is harmful, for we betray our own inner resolve to make our lives useful. By knowing that the Three Jewels are our best friends who will never abandon us, we'll always keep them in our hearts, no matter what external conditions we encounter.

All the above guidelines were set forth to help us make our lives meaningful. They are attitudes and actions that we train ourselves in gradually. It's wasted energy to feel we're guilty or bad because we don't follow these guidelines perfectly right now. Such self-judgment immobilizes us.

Instead, we can learn the guidelines and try to implement them as much as we can, reviewing them periodically to refresh our minds. We may choose one guideline to emphasize this week in our daily lives. Next week, we can add another, and so on. In that way, we'll slowly build up the good habits of practicing all of them.

# PRECEPTS:

*Directing our energy positively*

To help us direct our actions, word and thoughts positively, the Buddha outlined the ten destructive and the ten constructive actions . In addition, he set up three sets of vows or precepts. The first level of precepts are the precepts for individual liberation. These help us to refrain from doing destructive physical and verbal actions. The second level is the bodhisattva precepts, which help us subdue our self-cherishing attitude. The tantric precepts constitute the third level, and they work against the appearance and conception of things being ordinary and self-existent.

Precepts or vows are a joy, not a burden. They aren't designed to keep us from having a good time and to make us feel deprived. The purpose of taking precepts is to give us internal strength so we won't act in ways that we don't want to. Having understood that killing, stealing, selfishness and so forth only lead us to harm ourselves and others now and in the future, we'll want to avoid these. Taking precepts gives us energy and strength to do so. Therefore, it's said that precepts are the ornaments of the wise.

## Precepts for Individual Liberation

To help people overcome their disturbing attitudes and stop committing harmful actions, the Buddha set out five precepts. During a brief ceremony performed by a monk or nun, we can take refuge in the Triple Gem — Buddha, Dharma and Sangha. At the same time, we can take any or all of the five lay precepts, and become a lay follower — an *upasaka* (male) or *upasika* (female).

The five precepts, which are taken for life, are to avoid:

1.  taking the life of any being (killing),
2.  taking what is not given (stealing),
3.  unwise sexual behavior,

4. lying,
5. intoxicants.

When giving refuge, some teachers include only the first precept of not killing, and let us decide to take any or all of the other four. Other teachers give all five precepts at the time of giving refuge.

The first four actions have been described in the chapter, "The Four Noble Truths." The fifth precept is to abandon alcohol and intoxicating drugs. These substances are harmful because under their influence, we lose the ability to discriminate right and wrong. Under the influence of alcohol and drugs, people say cruel things to others and even beat their spouses and children.

Some people hesitate to take this precept for they worry about social occasions when everyone is expected to drink. I wonder how many people at a party or business function really want to drink. Maybe many drink because they think that everyone else expects them to, while in fact, no one wants to! Actually, it's not hard to refuse a drink. Everyone in the room won't stop and stare at us because we don't drink! In fact, we may be a good example for others who are too dependent on alcohol. In any case, we needn't be ashamed to act according to our principles.

There are different interpretations regarding tobacco. In the Theravada tradition smoking isn't prohibited by this precept, while in the Mahayana it is.

Coffee and tea may be taken. Although they have caffeine, they don't cause us to lose our senses. We can also take chilli and other spices.

Lay practitioners also may take eight precepts for a period of 24 hours. The first time we take these precepts, we must take them from someone else who has the lineage of the precepts, that is, who has taken the precepts from his or her master, who in turn has taken them from his or her master. In this way, the continuity of the precepts can be traced back to the Buddha.

Having first received the eight precepts from a qualified teacher, we can thereafter take them ourselves by imagining that we take them before all the Buddhas, bodhisattvas and arhats. The ceremony is brief, and must begin before dawn. The precepts last until dawn of the following day.

Many people like to take the eight precepts on new and full moon days or on Buddhist festivals, although they may be taken on any day. The first five of these eight are similar to the five lay precepts, with the exception that the precept against unwise sexual behavior becomes abstinence from sex, because the precepts are kept for only one day.

The sixth precept is to avoid wearing perfume, ornaments and cosmetics as well as to refrain from singing, dancing and playing music. This precept helps us avoid distractions to our practice. Not beautifying our body encourages us to cultivate our internal beauty of love, compassion and wisdom. If we sing and hum, then when we sit down to meditate, the tunes keep running through our minds.

The seventh precept is not to sit or sleep on a high or expensive bed or throne, as this could make us feel proud and superior to others.

The eighth precept is not to eat solid food after noon and to be vegetarian for the day. When some teachers give the eight precepts they say only lunch may be eaten, while other teachers allow both breakfast and lunch. Some teachers permit only water to be taken in the evening, others allow tea with a little milk, or fruit juice without pulp.

The purpose of this precept is to reduce attachment to food. It also enables us to meditate better in the evenings, for if we eat a big supper, often we feel heavy and sleepy.

Taking precepts has incredible benefit. Just think of how different our environment would be if everyone took just the first precept not to kill! The world would be a completely different place due to one precept. When we live with precepts, the lives of the people around us are immediately and dramatically affected: they live securely because of our firm intention not to harm them.

In addition, precepts make us increasingly aware of our actions, words and attitudes. They enable us to know ourselves better because we'll become aware of our habitual actions.

Also, having decided beforehand what actions we want to avoid, we don't get into a wishy-washy state of mind when we find ourselves in a situation in which we're tempted to do something we know we'll regret later.

Every moment that we are not actively transgressing a precept, we accumulate great positive potential, even if we're sleeping. The reason for this is that we have made a firm decision not to do that action and are actively not doing it. This accumulation of positive potential forms a firm base for attaining spiritual realizations, and creates the causal energy for us to die peacefully and have a fortunate rebirth.

If people would like to become even more mindful of their actions of body and speech, they may take the *sramanera* (male) or *sramanerika* (female) precepts. These are ten in number, although the Tibetan tradition spells out all their sub-classifications, making 36 in all. Often called the novice ordination, it's taken for life, and one becomes a monk or a nun.

After taking the novice ordination, monks and nuns may take the full ordination, becoming a *bhikshu* (male) or *bhikshuni* (female). The number of vows varies among different Buddhist lineages, and within each lineage, the *bhikshus* and *bhikshunis* have a different number of vows.

Traditionally, after taking the novice precepts and before taking the *bhikshuni* precepts, women take an intermediate ordination called *siksamana* that adds 12 more precepts onto those taken as a novice. Having held this ordination for two years, women may then take the full ordination. The lineages of all these ordinations have been passed down from teacher to student — without interruption from the time of the Buddha until today.

In the Theravada countries of Southeast Asia, however, the nuns' ordination died out several centuries ago. Today there are women in Sri Lanka with ten precepts called *dasasilmatas*. In Thailand there are women entitled *maejis* with eight precepts. But in both cases, their precepts are considered to be lay precepts, and they aren't officially regarded as ordained nuns. However, many women are looking into the possibility of bringing the *sramanerika*, *siksamana* and *bhikshuni* lineages from the Chinese tradition back into the Theravada tradition.

In Tibet, the novice ordination for women took root, but the *bhikshuni* ordination didn't. While the *sramanerika* ordination can be given by four *bhikshus* or *bhikshunis*, ten *bhikshunis* and *bhikshus* are required to give the *bhikshuni* ordination. It was difficult for women in those times to travel over the Himalaya Mountains, and thus the *bhikshuni* ordination didn't come to Tibet.

The Chinese Buddhists still continue the lineages for both the *bhikshu* and *bhikshuni* ordinations. Some women from the Theravada and Tibetan traditions have taken *bhikshuni* ordination from Chinese masters in recent years. People are now considering the possibility of reintroducing the *bhikshuni* ordination from Chinese Buddhism into the Theravada and Tibetan traditions.

In Japan, the monks' and nuns' precepts were altered during the Meiji Restoration in the mid-19th century, because the government wanted the ordained ones to marry. Thus in Japan, there are now both married and unmarried temple priests of both sexes, and the precepts they keep are enumerated differently from those of other Buddhist traditions.

Except for the eight precepts that are taken for one day, all other precepts are taken for the duration of the life. It may happen that due to unforeseen circumstances, a monk or a nun may not be able to keep the ordination any longer or may not wish to have it. In that case, he or she can go before a spiritual master, or even tell another person who can hear and understand, and return the precepts.

In Thailand there is a custom whereby most men become monks and hold the precepts for three months, at least once during their lives. They usually do this when they are young adults as it gives them a foundation in strict ethics and is very auspicious for their families. At the end of the three month period, they give back their precepts and return to family life.

All of these various precepts — those of the layman and laywoman and those of the various levels of monks and nuns — are included in what is broadly known as the *Pratimoksha*, or precepts for individual liberation. The basic motivation we must cultivate to take these is the determination to be free from cyclic existence. These precepts regulate our actions of body and speech, and are common to all the Buddhist traditions. No distinction among Theravada,

Mahayana or Vajrayana is made for the ordinations for individual liberation.

In the Mahayana tradition, there's the custom of taking the eight precepts after strongly generating an altruistic motivation. When we take the precepts in this way, they are called "the eight Mahayana precepts." While monks and nuns don't take the ordinary eight precepts for one day because they're included in their monks' and nuns' ordinations, they may take the eight Mahayana precepts.

## Bodhisattva Precepts

On the basis of refuge or any of the ordinations for individual liberation, we may then take the bodhisattva ordination. This is done not only with the determination to be free from cyclic existence, but also with the motivation of attaining enlightenment in order to benefit all beings. The bodhisattva vows work particularly to subdue the selfish attitude. They deal not only with our physical and verbal actions, but also with our thoughts and attitudes. Thus, they're more difficult to keep than the vows for individual liberation.

The bodhisattva ordination is found only in the Mahayana traditions. It may be taken by lay people, monks and nuns. Although the essence is the same, the enumeration of the precepts varies in the Tibetan and the Chinese versions. When taking these precepts, we determine to keep them until attaining enlightenment, although they certainly need to be renewed each lifetime!

The Chinese have the custom of burning incense on the heads of the monks and nuns or on the arms of the lay followers the evening before they take the bodhisattva precepts. This custom is unique to the Chinese and not done by the other Buddhist traditions. It's done by placing three small pieces of incense on the head or on the arm, lighting them and allowing them to burn into the skin. Some people may choose to have more than three pieces of incense. There's no difference in status between those with more or less.

Although this ritual may sound gruesome to some people, it isn't that painful. Perhaps this is because the temple is resonating with the chanting of the Buddha's name and people aren't concentrating on their own pain.

The significance of this ritual is three-fold. First, since the bodhisattva vows are taken with the motivation to attain enlightenment to benefit others, we must cultivate the courage to undergo suffering in the course of helping others. This isn't masochism, for we don't look for suffering. Rather, if we encounter bad circumstances in the process of working for others, we must be able to endure them. Enduring the pain of the incense burning into the skin signifies our courage and determination to help others no matter the cost to ourselves.

The second reason is to offer our bodies to the Buddha. Certainly, the Buddha doesn't ask us or need us to do this ritual to prove our devotion. Developed in China, the ritual signifies entrusting ourselves to the guidance of the Buddha. Generally, we're very attached and protective of our bodies. Here, that attachment is symbolically terminated by offering our bodies to the Buddha.

The third reason is a practical one. In ancient China, the monks and nuns weren't subjected to civil law as they were governed by the precepts and other monastic rules. However, neither the government nor the monasteries wanted common criminals to don the robes of ordained ones to escape punishment by civil law. Thus, this custom of burning incense on the monks and nuns' heads was instituted in China to demarcate the ordained from the unordained.

## Tantric Precepts

The third set of vows are the tantric precepts. Like the bodhisattva vows, these make us mindful of actions of body, speech and mind. They chiefly focus on eliminating the appearance and conceptions of things being both ordinary and inherently existent, which prevent us from attaining enlightenment. The tantric vows are the most difficult to keep purely. However, the benefit from maintaining them is also greater.

Tantric vows are taken during some tantric initiations, and thus are found only in the Vajrayana tradition, which is a branch of the

Mahayana. To take them, we must have taken refuge, some or all of the vows for individual liberation, and the bodhisattva vows. We pledge to keep the tantric vows until we attain enlightenment.

## Taking Precepts

Taking any of the three sets of vows is entirely voluntary. To take them, we must understand the advantages of living ethically. There are innumerable benefits, but they may be subsumed by saying that living ethically leads us to liberation and enlightenment and enables us to make our lives useful for others.

Some people hesitate to take precepts because they feel they can't keep them purely. But we shouldn't expect ourselves to be perfect from the outset. If we could protect our precepts without one blemish, we needn't take them, because we'd already be an arhat or a Buddha. Precepts are taken because we can't keep them perfectly. But through trying to, our actions, speech and attitudes will improve.

Still we shouldn't take precepts if we're completely incapable of maintaining them. That would be foolish! We need a balanced attitude. It's like a child wanting to eat a piece of fruit. If she doesn't eat it because she's afraid it's too big, she'll miss out on something that's good for her. If she tries to put it in her mouth all at one time, she'll choke. But, by taking the amount that can fit in her mouth, she'll grow. Similarly, we should take precepts according to our ability to practice them.

To keep our precepts, we need to be very conscientious and mindful. Should we transgress them, we can employ the four opponent powers — regret, refuge and the altruistic intention, remedial action and the determination not to repeat the negative action — to purify the imprints left on our mindstreams. These four were described in a previous chapter, during the discussion of karma.

Precepts are regarded as the ornaments of a sincere practitioner. Even if we don't wish to take precepts, the effect of abandoning the ten destructive actions is immediately felt in our lives. The people around us notice the difference in our behavior and come to trust and respect us more. Our minds are calmer, and we can concentrate when we meditate. Ethical conduct is indeed the foundation of all temporal and ultimate happiness. As the Buddha said:

Sandalwood, *tagara*, lotus and jasmine:
Above all these fragrances
The perfume of virtue
Is by far the best.

# III

# THE SPREAD OF THE BUDDHA'S TEACHINGS

*In the preceding sections, we looked at the essence of the Buddha's teachings and how they apply to our lives in the 20th century. But we may wonder what its origins were and how it was passed down in a pure form to our day. Why are there many Buddhist traditions and what are they? How is Buddhism practiced in various countries? These will be discussed in this section.*

# THE LIFE OF THE BUDDHA:

*An inspiration for us all*

He gave expression to truths of everlasting value and advanced the ethics not of India alone but of humanity. Buddha was one of the greatest ethical men of genius ever bestowed upon the world.
*Albert Schweitzer, French scholar, theologian, philosopher and winner of the Nobel Prize*

The lives of truly remarkable people improve society so greatly that we're grateful they lived. In addition, their biographies inspire us and show us how we too can transverse hardships and benefit others. In the Buddha's life story, we find circumstances that we can identify with and relate to our lives and our efforts to become better people.

The Buddha was born a prince in the Shakya royal family of Kapilavastu in modern-day Nepal, around 560 B.C. His mother had several auspicious dreams before his birth, and as a newborn, he is said to have taken seven steps and declared, "This shall be my last rebirth."

Some people find great joy in hearing about the many miraculous occurrences that surround the Buddha's birth and life and that demonstrate his spiritual achievements. Other people are skeptical about these accounts for such things haven't been scientifically explained yet.

We could debate endlessly about this, but to do so is to miss the point. What's important is that we improve the quality of our lives by following a correct path. Hearing the life story of another person should be an inspiration and example for our own spiritual growth. Thus, if you find the stories of miraculous events inspirational and helpful in your life, that's good. If you don't, that's fine too. Concentrate on the parts of the life story that have meaning for you.

The Buddha's mother died a week after his birth, and he was raised by his stepmother, Prajapati. A wise man told the Buddha's father, the king of Kapilavastu, that the child would be an exceptional personage — either a great king with political, economic and social power, or a great sage with the wisdom and compassion to lead others on the spiritual path.

The king wanted the best for his child, and in his eyes, that meant having power over people and wealth. He didn't see the value of his child being religious. Thus the king created what he considered the best possible environment for his child's growth — one in which the child, Siddhartha, had everything that money could buy. Anything disagreeable was excluded from the child's environs, and he was not allowed beyond the palace walls, for there he might contact something unpleasant.

As a child, Siddhartha was very compassionate and successful in both intellectual pursuits and athletics. He married well and had a child. In all ways he fulfilled the expectations of his family and society, and was what they would call "a success."

One day, he ventured beyond the protected environment of the palace with his charioteer. There he saw an old person — wrinkled, frail, bent over, and in pain. This was a new sight for the sheltered prince, since elderly people had been banned from the palace. When he questioned the charioteer about this person, he learned that the aging process happens to all of us, without choice. Returning to the palace, he was melancholy, his dream bubble of perfect worldly happiness shattered by the first pinprick.

Another day he ventured out with the charioteer, this time seeing a sick person on the street. Again, upon asking, he learned that all of us are subject to illness, although we don't desire it.

The third time he went out, he saw a corpse. When the charioteer explained that death is inevitable and all of us must leave our bodies, enjoyments and loved ones, the prince was horrified. He was beginning to wonder what life was all about, considering that without choice, we experience aging, sickness and death. What use were all his beautiful possessions, his power and prestige, if they couldn't prevent these? He realized that even his family and friends, though they loved him immensely, could prevent neither his sickness, aging and death, nor their own.

On the fourth excursion outside the palace walls, he saw a mendicant dressed in simple clothes, with few possessions. The charioteer explained that this was someone who had left behind the distractions of family life and was seeking the meaning of life and the solution to its problems.

One evening after a gala affair, after having seen even the beautiful dancing girls asleep, snoring, with their hair disheveled, Siddhartha decided he had to seek a solution to the dissatisfactory nature of life. He saw no sense in devoting his life to pleasures of the senses if one day he must die and leave them all, never having actualized his full potential as a human being.

He kissed his sleeping wife and child good-bye, and with his charioteer, left the palace. Discarding his exquisite royal clothes and jewelry, he donned simple garb and cut his hair. Seeking to learn the answer to life's mysteries, he went in search of a teacher.

For some years he studied with the most renowned meditation masters of his time, and achieved perfection in all they taught. Still, his mind wasn't free from attachment, anger and ignorance. To change this, he decided to follow a path of extreme ascetic practices. With five companions, he meditated for six years, eating only one grain of rice each day. Although he attained high states of *samadhi*, his mind still wasn't completely free. He learned through his own experience that torturing the body wasn't the source of spiritual realizations.

## Enlightenment

Giving up extreme asceticism, he regained his physical strength and went to Bodh Gaya, in northeastern India. There, he sat beneath a bodhi tree and vowed not to arise until perfect enlightenment had been attained.

Then, tradition says that Mara, the chief of the demons, sent his forces to disrupt Siddhartha's meditation. We may regard Mara as an external being who creates hindrances, or as that part of our own minds that is still confused, clinging and unclear. The story of the ensuing battle has many messages for us.

Mara first sent aggressive warriors to disrupt Siddhartha, but the meditator transformed their weapons into a rain of flowers. This means that the fear and anger in our minds can be conquered by love.

Mara next sent his daughters, voluptuous and enchanting, to lure the bodhisattva from his resolve and disturb his concentration. However, Siddhartha transformed them into hideous hags who fled in humiliation. Our desires have no strength when we look beyond the superficial appearance of what we're attached to.

Lastly, Mara challenged the bodhisattva's right to be there, questioning if he had enough positive potential. Siddhartha touched the ground, and the goddess of the earth appeared, testifying to his great accumulation of positive potential. This shows that our doubt is dispelled when we're firmly grounded in reality. Defeated, Mara departed.

During the night, the bodhisattva continued to meditate, gradually removing the last vestiges of the stains of ignorance and self-ishness, and at dawn, he became a fully enlightened Buddha, one who has cleansed all defilements from his mind and who has developed all good qualities to their fullest.

At first the Buddha appeared hesitant to teach, for would anyone understand the extraordinary experience he had had? Then the great celestial beings, headed by Brahma, came to request him to teach, saying surely there were people with little dust on their wisdom-eyes who could benefit.

The Buddha journeyed to Sarnath, where he knew his five companions, the ascetics, were. Seeing him, they were disgusted that he had relinquished his asceticism, and they vowed to ignore him. However, as the Buddha drew nearer, their preconceptions and anger dissolved in the face of his radiant compassion and wisdom. They welcomed him, and he gave his first teaching.

This first discourse was on the four truths. The ascetics gained understanding of them, requested ordination, and eventually became arhats. In this way, the Sangha community was formed.

For 45 years, the Buddha traveled throughout northern India, teaching and giving counsel. People from all walks of life became his disciples and benefited immensely from practicing what he taught. At one point he returned to Kapilavastu and taught the Dharma to his family. His father, now understanding the benefit of his son's spiritual practice, was pleased with him and learned from him. The Buddha's son became a monk.

After the demise of his father, the Buddha's stepmother together with 500 Shakya women requested ordination. At first the Buddha refused, probably because he didn't want his stepmother to make such a decision due to her grief at the loss of her husband.

Prajapati was determined, however. She and the 500 other women, followed the Buddha the many long miles to Vaisali, shaved their heads and donned the saffron robes to show their sincerity. Ananda, the Buddha's attendant, questioned the Buddha whether women were able to become arhats, and the Buddha responded that they were. The Buddha decided to grant them ordination, and the order of nuns was formed. The Buddha's wife later became a nun too.

# The Social Impact of Buddhism

In many ways the Buddha was a social revolutionary of his time. He spoke strongly against ritual for ritual's sake, thus forcing people to consider the purpose of the Brahminical rituals they performed. He also spoke out against the discrimination and prejudice of the caste system, and didn't allow it within the Sangha community. He insisted that all people be treated equally. Respect was to be given to those who had been ordained longer and those with realizations, not those who were born into a certain social class.

Considering the inferior position of women in ancient Indian society, the Buddha shocked many people by acknowledging women's spiritual capacity. He allowed women to leave the home, where, according to societal custom, they were always under the care and custody of men: first their fathers, then their husbands, and in old age their sons.

There were many eminent nuns who attained arhatship, and their teachings are in the scripture entitled *The Therigatha.* Some people say that the Buddha initially declined to ordain women and then reluctantly changed his mind, implying that maybe he made a mistake. However, the Buddha also declined to teach the Dharma at first and later changed his mind. No one says that he made a mistake by doing that!

Also, contrary to the authoritarian governments that existed in India at that time, the Buddha favored a more republican and democratic system, which he instituted in the Sangha community. After monks and nuns were ordained for ten years, they were considered stable in their practices and were designated "elders." The elders met together to discuss, form and enforce policies in the Sangha communities.

The "law" of the Sangha community was the monks' and nuns' vows set down by the Buddha. When the first disciples took ordination, there were no specific vows. The precepts came into being as some monks and nuns acted in ways that either harmed themselves or others or were offensive to others. When such a situation was brought to the Buddha's attention, he would then say that in the future, his ordained disciples should refrain from such an action.

The principal vows are not to kill a human being, steal, lie about one's spiritual attainments or have sexual relations. Other vows regulate the monks' and nuns' physical appearance and dress, behavior with other monks and nuns, and etiquette. The Sangha also are not to take intoxicants of any kind.

The Buddha had many lay disciples from all classes, as well as the communities of monks and nuns. The relationship between the ordained and the lay was one of mutual benefit and appreciation. The "job" of the Sangha community was to practice the teachings as well as it could, to be an inspirational example to others, and to teach and guide others. To do this, the monks and nuns were to live a simple life. They were not to engage in agriculture or business for their livelihood, because these occupations require a lot of time that could be used for study and meditation, and they could also arouse attachment.

Therefore, each morning the monks and nuns went on alms rounds to collect their daily food at the homes of the laity. Although this has sometimes been translated as "begging," it isn't. The monks and nuns wouldn't ask for food, nor was anyone obliged to give it to them. They would silently pass the homes, and those people who saw value in the Sangha's spiritual pursuits and wanted to help them, happily gave to them.

The ordained ones were not parasites on society. In fact, they had a crucial role to play in it, for they practiced the teachings, and by integrating the Dharma in their mindstreams, they improved their conduct and wisdom. They could then teach these methods to the laity, as well as demonstrate that it's possible to become more peaceful, compassionate and open people.

Nevertheless, that doesn't mean that because people are ordained, their behavior is automatically impeccable. They are training. Most Buddhists — whether they are ordained or lay — are not yet Buddhas! They are trying to become enlightened. Although the path that the Buddha described is perfect, the humans who practice it aren't always that way.

When the Buddha was 80, after 45 years of teaching and guiding others, he passed away at Kusinagara. This is also called the Buddha's *parinirvana*. Rather than appoint a successor and establish a hierarchy, the Buddha encouraged his followers to let the Dharma — the teachings he gave — be their guide. In doing this, he emphasized the importance of each individual's sincere practice, and expressed his wish that the Sangha live together democratically.

# BUDDHIST TRADITIONS:

*Finding what suits our personality*

In the first rainy-season after the *parinirvana,* the First Council was held at Rajagrha. The 500 arhats who attended recited and compiled the sutras — the teachings given by the Buddha. For several centuries after that, the sutras were memorized and passed down orally to each succeeding generation.

The Buddha spoke to a wide range of people from every social, educational and economic background. His followers varied in disposition, interest and inclination. Thus, the Buddha taught according to the specific group present at each discourse, using words and concepts suitable for them.

The various teachings he gave developed into two principal traditions: the Theravada and the Mahayana. The Theravada contains the teachings spoken by the Buddha to people who were interested in being free from cyclic existence and attaining liberation. These sutras were passed down orally until the first century B.C., when they were written down in Ceylon and became what is known as the Pali Canon.

The Mahayana teachings were given by the Buddha to an audience with strong interest in the bodhisattva's path to Buddhahood. After the Buddha's passing away, the Mahayana teachings weren't practiced publicly, but were passed down privately from teacher to student. Tradition has it that some Mahayana sutras were taken to another land to be cared for until conditions were right for their widespread propagation in our world. From the first century B.C. onwards, the Mahayana sutras began to appear publicly, and this way of practice became more widely known.

The Mahayana has two methods of practice, Paramitayana and Vajrayana. Paramitayana is the general bodhisattva path found in the sutras, and it emphasizes the altruistic intention and the practice of the six far-reaching attitudes. Ch'an (Zen), Pure Land and others are included in the Paramitayana. Vajrayana contains the Theravada and Paramitayana methods and adds the practice of meditating on various manifestations of the Buddhas (Buddhist meditational deties). Vajrayana techniques are found in teachings the Buddha gave called the tantras.

Buddhism is remarkably flexible in the external forms it takes. Thus, it has adapted to the culture of each country where it has taken root. While the Buddhist traditions vary in terms of which texts they chiefly rely on, which practice they emphasize, and the outward manifestations of the practice, they are all united in that they are the teachings of a very skillful and wise teacher, the Buddha.

The various traditions maintain the purity of the Buddha's doctrine. This is important, because to progress along the path we must follow it correctly. It would be very harmful to change the teachings, for that would amount to making up our own path to enlightenment, rather than following the guidance of someone who has already achieved it.

When first coming to Buddhism, some people are bewildered by the variety of Buddhist traditions. In the next few chapters, we'll look at the major traditions existing today, and how they developed historically. As this is a vast subject, only the most prominent traditions are discussed: Theravada, Pure Land, Ch'an (Zen) and Tibetan Buddhism.

We may personally be more attracted to one tradition and focus upon it. However, we can't say this tradition is better than the others, or that it's the most suitable for everyone else. Such sectarianism is extremely harmful. Instead, we should appreciate Buddhism even more because it acknowledges and accepts everyone's different dispositions, interests and cultures.

# THERAVADA, TRADITION OF THE ELDERS:

*Buddhism in Sri Lanka and Southeast Asia*

Saffron-robed monks, fragrant flower offerings in temples, melodious chanting in Pali and the deep peace of silent meditation — these are images evoked by the Theravada tradition.

The Theravada tradition was widely practiced in India after the Buddha's passing away. By the 3rd century B.C., it was established in current-day Pakistan and Afghanistan, and took root in Central Asia in the early centuries A.D. Muslim invasions in the 11th and 12th centuries virtually extinguished the religion in the Indian sub-continent and in Central Asia.

In the third century B.C., King Ashok of India sent missionaries to Ceylon (Sri Lanka), where Buddhism became firmly established. The Theravada tradition still flourishes there. From India and from Ceylon, it spread to Southeast Asia, and is presently strong in Thailand and Burma. The present communist governments of several other countries in Southeast Asia have suppressed Buddhism. In recent years the Theravada tradition has become more widely practiced in Malaysia and Singapore.

In the 19th century, Western intellectuals became interested in the Theravada tradition. Nowadays, it attracts people from all walks of life and Theravada monasteries, Dharma centers and retreat sites have been established throughout the West.

Based on the Pali Canon, the Theravada tradition presents Buddha's teachings by first explaining the four noble truths, the three higher trainings and the noble eight-fold path. These have been discussed in previous chapters.

The Theravada tradition states that the number of people who can become Buddhas are very few. In our eon, there will be 1000 Buddhas, of which Shakyamuni Buddha is the fourth. The 996 Buddhas-to-be are now bodhisattvas. Thus, as the rest of us won't become Buddhas, we should aim to become arhats, those who are free from cyclic existence and have attained nirvana. (The difference between Buddhas and arhats was explained in "The Four Noble Truths.")

People wishing to attain nirvana should take refuge and the five lay precepts. They can also take monastic vows. In the Theravada tradition full monastic ordination is considered an important condition for the attainment of nirvana.

There is a considerable difference between Sangha and lay people in their way of practicing the Dharma in Asian Theravada countries. The monks keep their precepts purely, study, meditate and dedicate the positive potential they create for everyone's welfare. Because the Sangha's practice benefits society as a whole, the laity happily supply daily requisites — food, clothing, shelter and medicine — to the monks.

This view of the roles of Sangha and lay is changing as the Theravada tradition takes root in the West. Most Western lay Buddhists are interested in meditation and many meditate daily before and after going to work. They go to Dharma centers for their annual vacation. Some even take several months leave from their jobs to participate in lengthy retreats. In the West, Dharma teachers are both ordained and lay, men and women.

## The Theravada Method of Practice

The more I studied *satipathana* (mindfulness meditation), the more impressed I became with it as a system of mind training. It is in line with our Western scientific attitude of mind in that it is unprejudiced, objective and analytical. It relies on personal, direct experience, and not on anyone else's ideas or opinions....it gets you out of the rut and bondage of yourself, your prejudices, your cliches, your blindness and your self-opinionatedness, to set you free to see and prove a real world.
*Dr. E. Graham Howe, MB. BS. DPM., eminent British physician*

In all Buddhist traditions, two principal qualities are developed in meditation: *samatha* (calm abiding) and *vipassana* (special insight). Generally, calm abiding is practiced first to free the mind from its internal chatter and to develop concentration. In the Theravada tradition, the breath is taken as the object of meditation, and one trains the mind to be alert and focused on the sensation of the breath in each moment.

When initially trying to concentrate, the mind is cluttered with mental noise, like being trapped in a room with 15 radios, all blaring on different stations. Several techniques are applied to help solve this problem. One may relax each part of the body, and while doing so, let go of a distracting thought. In another technique, one simply acknowledges the presence of the thoughts and emotions which arise, but doesn't give them attention and energy. In this way, they settle of their own accord. Another technique instructs one to recite the syllables "Bud dha" on the in- and out-breaths to help focus one's concentration.

Apart from formal sitting meditation, one does walking meditation. Walking slowly, one concentrates on each movement and sensation involved in lifting, moving, and placing the feet. In fact, in all daily actions sitting, standing, lying down, talking or whatever — one tries to be aware of each minute action and event.

By focusing the mind on the sensation of the breath in sitting meditation and on each movement in walking meditation, one becomes more aware of the richness of the present moment. In addition, one's concentration is removed from the daydreams and barrage of thoughts that feed the disturbing attitudes. The mind remains tranquil, and one fully experiences every event in life.

The practice of special insight, or *vipassana*, develops an acutely perceptive and discerning state of mind that can directly perceive the ultimate reality, selflessness or lack of an solid self-identity. In the Theravada practice, this is done by means of the four mindfulnesses (*satipathana*): mindfulness of the body, feelings, mind and phenomena.

Closely examining these four, one becomes aware of three characteristics: their transience, their problematic or suffering nature, and their lack of a solid self-identity. By observing and examining the breath, the feelings in the body, the various consciousnesses, and the mental factors in each moment, one realizes there is no little person somewhere inside one's head running the show. We are selfless, without a solid self-identity that needs to be pleased and protected.

Special insight is also developed outside of formal sitting meditation. By being acutely aware of each action, feeling and thought, one examines who is doing and experiencing these things. Finding only a continuous stream of mental and physical events, without a concrete personality or self who is the boss, one understands selflessness.

Combining special insight with the concentration of calm abiding, one is able to cleanse the mindstream of all disturbing attitudes and the karma that cause suffering. Attaining liberation, one becomes an arhat.

The meditation on loving-kindness, or *metta*, is also popular in the Theravada tradition. One begins by thinking, "May I be well and happy," and gradually spreads this good feeling to friends, strangers and enemies. Considering each in turn, one thinks, "May they be well and happy." One must let these words resonate inside oneself so they become one's own attitude. Calm abiding can also be developed through meditation on loving-kindness.

In the West, Theravada practice is popular with people who wish to calm their uncontrolled thoughts and emotions and to focus on positive attitudes. Many people in the business world have found breathing meditation extremely helpful in this respect. Meditation on loving-kindness has helped them improve relationships with their families and colleagues. This 2,500-year-old tradition is certainly applicable and beneficial today!

# MAHAYANA: BUDDHISM IN THE FAR EAST

*A look at Pure Land and Zen*

Buddhism first came to China from Central Asia in the first century A.D. Later, it was brought from India by both sea and land routes. By the fourth century, *bhikshu* and *bhikshuni* ordination lineages were established in China. In following centuries, Chinese pilgrims continued to bring a wealth of Buddhist texts from India to China.

Pre-Buddhist China was influenced by the indigenous philosophies of Confucianism and Taoism. When it entered China, Buddhism was flexible and adapted its external forms to the existing culture. For example, Confucianism emphasized etiquette, respect for elders and teachers, filial piety and proper behavior. When Buddhism came to China, the monks emphasized the sutra on the kindness of the parents, as this complemented values important in Chinese culture. Similarly, etiquette and formal ceremonial procedures were stressed in Buddhist monasteries.

Taoist practice contained breathing exercises and techniques to develop the subtle energies of the body. *Chigong*, a system of exercises working with energies in the body, also had existed in China for many centuries. The Buddha had taught breathing exercises and meditation to control the body's subtle energies as well. Thus when the Indian meditation master Bodhidharma went to China, he improved upon the already existing practices there and developed a set of exercises to improve the monks' health. In this way, the martial arts' exercises came to be practiced in Buddhist monasteries. However, contrary to popular films, Buddhist monks didn't spend their days flipping opponents over their shoulders! They engaged principally in the study and practice of Buddha's teachings.

The Buddhist texts brought to China by Indian missionaries and Chinese pilgrims weren't initially systematized. Over time, people became unsure how to resolve seeming discrepancies between sutras, and how to practice the teachings in this vast amount of literature.

Thus, in the seventh century there were spontaneous attempts to organize the Buddhist teachings in China. Groups grew up around various monks, each of whom chose a particular sutra or group of sutras as the central point of their study and practice. These groups later evolved and became Buddhist traditions, each one passed down by a lineage of masters. Eight major traditions developed in China, as well as some minor ones. The eight principal traditions were:

1. San-lun, which followed the Madhyamika (Middle Way) philosophical school of Indian Buddhism.

2. Fa-hsiang, which followed the Yogacara (Cittamatrin, Mind Only) philosophical school of Indian Buddhism.

3. Satyasiddhi (Ch'eng-shih), a Theravada tradition.

4. Hua-yen, which was based on the *Avatamsaka Sutra* and dealt with an array of metaphysical concepts for contemplation.

5. T'ien-t'ai, which took the *Lotus Sutra* as foremost and presented a balance between meditation, philosophical study, and good deeds.

6. Third Period (San-chieh-chiao), a method for purification based on strict observance of monastic vows and charitable actions.

7. Ch'an (Jap., Zen), which emphasized meditation and the *Lankavatara Sutra*.

8. Pure Land, in which practitioners strove to be reborn in the pure lands of Amitabha Buddha or Maitreya Buddha.

Aside from these eight major traditions, Chen-yen (True Word), a tantric tradition, existed in China in the eighth and ninth centuries.

In the Great T'ang Persecution of 842-845 A.D., Buddhism was severely repressed in China. All of the traditions except for Ch'an and Pure Land were essentially destroyed, although their influence remains and there is interest in them today. After 845, Ch'an and Pure Land became the principal Buddhist traditions, both of them studying the Middle Way and Mind Only philosophies. Since the 16th century, Ch'an and Pure Land practices have been blended together in many Chinese monasteries.

From China, Mahayana Buddhism spread to Vietnam beginning in the second century A.D. and to Korea in the fourth century. Ch'an became prevalent in both places, although in Vietnam Pure Land and Theravada traditions became popular as well.

In the sixth century, most Chinese Buddhist traditions reached Japan via Korea. In the 12th and 13th centuries, many new traditions proliferated in Japan. This occurred because people were bewildered by the vastness of the Buddha's teachings and sought a single effective practice to engage in.

During this time, two Pure Land traditions branched off from the T'ien-t'ai tradition. Of these, the Jodo-shin-shu, the True Pure Land Sect, emphasized the family as the center of religious life. It began the custom of married priests, who take vows and lead religious practices in temples. The temples are passed down from father to eldest son.

Although Ch'an (Zen) came to Japan as early as the seventh century, it became popular in the 12th. Many Zen traditions exist, but Rinzai and Soto became the most well-known.

In the 13th century, the Nichiren tradition, based on the *Lotus Sutra*, appeared. Shingon, the Japanese tantric tradition, was also re-vitalized around this time.

In the Meiji Restoration of 1868, the Japanese government decreed that all Buddhist clergy be allowed to marry. During the Japanese occupation of Korea in the early 20th century, non-celibate priesthood was introduced. But now most Korean Sangha follow the ordination vows of monks and nuns, which necessarily include celibacy.

Post-war Japan has seen the arisal of many small groups, each with its own way of practice. Some have integrated the pre-Buddhist Shinto beliefs into their system, others have adopted a Christian bent. If we're interested in Buddhist practice, we should examine well the teachings of these groups to determine if their interpretation is faithful to the Buddha's teachings.

From Japan in particular, Zen and Nichiren-shu have spread to Western countries. Zen has become very popular in the West, where people attend meditation sessions and retreats. Some Zen centers have begun social welfare programs as well: hospices to help the terminally ill or people with AIDS.

Having seen the historical development of Buddhism in East Asia, let's look at the two most prominent traditions there: Ch'an (Zen) and Pure Land.

# Pure Land

The melodious and soothing chant of "Namo Amito Fo" (Homage to Amitabha Buddha) resonates in many Chinese temples and homes. The figures of Amitabha, flanked by his two chief attendants, the bodhisattvas Avalokiteshvara and Mahasthamaprapta, inspire many. For centuries the simplicity of the Pure Land practice, which centers upon the recitation of Amitabha's name, has attracted devotees from all classes of society.

The Pure Land tradition is rooted in the *Sukhavati-vyuha Sutra,* as well as several other sutras describing how to be reborn in Amitabha's pure land, Sukhavati (Blissful Pure Land or Western Paradise). The Amitabha practice existed in India, although it wasn't as prominent there as in East Asia. In the second century A.D., the *Sukhavati-vyuha Sutra* was translated into Chinese, and in the early sixth century it became very popular.

This practice fit in very well with Chinese culture. Taoist practice revolved around attaining longevity, and since Amitabha Buddha is the same as Amitayus, Buddha of Infinite Life, people became interested in the Pure Land practice. Similarly, the Taoist concern with longevity was transferred to seeking rebirth in Amitabha's Pure Land. The practice of reciting *dharani* (efficacious syllables) was already popular in northern China, making it easy for people to switch to chanting Amitabha's name.

These conditions enabled people to easily adopt the Pure Land practice. In addition, times were hard in China, and people welcomed a technique which was simple and direct. Pure Land wasn't presented as an elitist practice, but one that everyone, the illiterate as well as the scholarly, could participate in.

The long-term goal of this practice is to attain enlightenment for the benefit of all beings. The immediate goal is to be reborn in Sukhavati, the Blissful Pure Land, in the next life. This pure land is not included in the six realms of cyclic existence because once beings are born there, they'll definitely attain enlightenment and will never be reborn in cyclic existence again. Of course, once people become Buddhas in Sukhavati, they'll manifest in our world to lead others to enlightenment.

Why is rebirth in a pure land desirable? In the human world, sincere practitioners often face many obstacles: they have to work long hours and thus have less time for concentrated practice; there is crime and anger in society; people have to worry about money to support their families; distractions from the media lure their attention away from practice.

In the pure lands such as Sukhavati, these hindrances don't exist. Everyone practices Dharma, and all the conditions — physical, social, economic, etc. — are conducive to realizing the path. Because attaining enlightenment is easy there, rebirth in Sukhavati desirable. In addition, Sukhavati is unusual among the many pure lands because it's easier to go there: ordinary beings who have neither direct perception of emptiness nor full-fledged altruistic intention (bodhicitta) can be reborn there.

Sukhavati Pure Land came into existence as a result of the practice of a bodhisattva monk, Dharmakara, who many eons ago had the wish to create a place where other beings could easily practice Dharma. He made a series of vows in which he promised to establish this pure land when he became a Buddha and described the means by which others could be reborn there. Dharmakara then learned the Dharma from a previous Buddha, generated the altruistic intention, and completed the practices of calm abiding and special insight. In this way, he became the Buddha Amitabha, and by the power of his positive potential and wisdom, Sukhavati came into being.

How can people be reborn in Sukhavati? Some people believe that having strong faith in Amitabha and reciting his name are sufficient. Then, by Amitabha's power, they'll be led to the pure land when they die.

This is a rather simplistic view and raises the question, "Buddha said no one can save us but ourselves. We must practice Dharma and transform our own minds. Isn't it contradictory to say one needs only to have faith and Amitabha will do the rest?"

Yes, this is contradictory. While Amitabha can inspire and guide people, they must practice. The Sukhavati sutras set out this practice: ethical conduct, purification of destructive actions, generation of the altruistic intention, concentration and meditation on the qualities of the Buddha and the Pure Land. Then, with a heart-felt aspiration, one dedicates the positive potential from one's practice to be reborn in Sukhavati in order to attain enlightenment for the benefit of all others.

Faith is an adjunct to meditation. It arises not through blind belief or desperation, but through knowing the qualities of the Buddhas, Dharma and Sangha.

The practice of reciting Amitabha's name can be used to develop the above qualities. For example, by reciting "Namo Amito Fo" while thinking of Amitabha's altruistic intention, one admires the bodhicitta and will develop it in one's life. By focusing on the sound of Amitabha's name, one eliminates distractions and develops concentration. One can gain calm abiding (*samatha*) by using a visualized image of Amitabha and the pure land as one's meditation object. Special insight (*vipassana*) on selflessness is developed by meditating on the emptiness of inherent existence of Amitabha and oneself. Thus we see the Pure Land practice is very rich and goes beyond merely reciting Amitabha's name.

During daily life activities one continues the recitation to remind oneself of the qualities of the Three Jewels. While walking or driving, one can develop mindfulness on the sound of Amitabha's name. Remembering that ethical conduct is a principal cause for rebirth in a pure land, one becomes mindful of what one thinks, says and does.

Some of the confusion about whether recitation of Amitabha's name is sufficient practice arose because the Chinese term "nien-fo" has several meanings. "Nien" can mean: 1) concentration or meditation, 2) a moment of time, 3) vocal recitation. In India, Amitabha practice centered upon meditation. In China, it emphasized recitation of his name. The same Chinese term could be applied to both.

Also, when masters stress the importance of relying on Amitabha, one shouldn't think Amitabha is an all-powerful god who can do everything. According to Buddhism, a Buddha is omniscient, but not omnipotent. It's impossible for anyone to be omnipotent. The power of a Buddha and the power of sentient beings' karma are equal. If one hasn't created the cause to be reborn in Sukhavati by doing positive actions, Amitabha can't magically make one go there.

There are various ways to regard Amitabha, according to the

level of one's understanding and practice. The external Buddha Amitabha resides in the pure land. However, the internal Buddha Amitabha is the enlightened mind that our present mind can transform into by practicing the Dharma. Neither the external nor the internal Amitabha is a concrete, findable personality. In fact, the more one understands selflessness, the more one has a proper understanding of who Amitabha is.

As with all Buddhist practices, this one can be done on several levels, depending upon the understanding of the practitioner. Recitation and generating devotion to Amitabha is beneficial for people who lack education or who don't have the time or interest to learn Buddhist philosophy. For them, it provides direction in their lives and refuge during stressful times. By reciting Amitabha's name and thinking of him, they create positive potential. People with a more comprehensive understanding of the Buddhist path to enlightenment, apply this to the Pure Land practice, and thus attain profound realizations.

The Pure Land tradition is well-suited for people who find devotion inspires them to abandon disturbing attitudes and develop their good qualities. Invigorated by their confidence in Amitabha, they'll practice the Dharma and gain the realizations of Amitabha in their own mindstreams.

# Ch'an (Zen)

Zen is traced to a teaching the Buddha gave by silently holding up a golden lotus. The general audience was perplexed, but the disciple Mahakasyapa understood the significance and smiled subtly. The implication of this is that the essence of the Dharma is beyond words. In Zen, that essence is transmitted from teacher to disciple in sudden moments, breakthroughs of understanding.

The meaning Mahakasyapa understood was passed down in a lineage of 28 Indian patriarchs to Bodhidharma. Bodhidharma, an Indian meditation master, strongly adhered to the *Lankavatara Sutra,* a Yogacara text. He went to China around 470 A.D., and began the

Ch'an tradition there. It spread to Korea and Vietnam, and in the 12th century became popular in Japan.

Ch'an in Sanskrit is "dhyana," which means meditative concentration. All the early Indian missionaries and Chinese monks were meditation masters. Meditation was one of many practices the Buddha gave instruction in — ethics, generosity, patience and wisdom were others — and the Ch'an tradition arose from some practitioners' wish to make meditation their focal point.

An underlying principle in Zen is that all beings have Buddha nature, the seed of intrinsic Buddhahood. Some Zen masters express this by saying all beings are already Buddhas, but their minds are clouded over by disturbing attitudes and obscurations. Their job, then, is to perceive this Buddha nature and let it shine forth without hindrance.

Because the fundamental requirement for Buddhahood — Buddha nature — is already within everyone, Zen stresses attaining enlightenment in this lifetime. Zen masters don't teach about rebirth and karma in depth, although they accept these.

According to Zen, there is no need to avoid the world by seeking nirvana elsewhere. This is because first, all beings have Buddha nature already, and second, when they realize emptiness, they'll see that cyclic existence and nirvana are not different.

Zen is acutely aware of the limitations of language, and gears its practice to transcend it. Experience is stressed, not mere intellectual learning. Thus, associating with an experienced teacher is important. The Zen teacher's duty is to bring the students back to the reality existing in the present moment whenever their fanciful minds get involved in conceptual wanderings. This is illustrated by lively anecdotes of Zen masters catching their students offguard and thus breaking through the confusion of their unrealistic views.

*Sanzen*, daily consultation with the teacher, is conducted during periods of intense meditation. Brief but to-the-point discussion with the spiritual master can not only trigger insight in the student, but also gives the teacher the opportunity to access and validate the student's experiences in meditation. Having a profound personal relationship also provides for the mind-to-mind transmission of Dharma experience from teacher to student.

Zazen, sitting meditation, is a key practice. The two major Zen traditions, Soto and Rinzai, have a slightly different approach to this. Soto Zen teaches "just sitting" in which one focuses on the nature of the mind. Soto emphasizes "original enlightenment," and doesn't distinguish between the means and the end. Instead of constantly trying to achieve something, one is encouraged to just be, and to be aware of that.

Calm abiding is developed in Soto Zen by just sitting, thus concentrating the mind single-pointedly. Based on confidence that sitting is the perfect expression of inherent perfection or enlightenment, the practice of special insight involves total awareness of the body sitting in each moment .

Rinzai Zen employs the koan (Chinese, *kung-an*) to develop special insight. Different koans are used by each teacher, and each koan serves a different purpose. But basically, these short puzzles, such as "What was the appearance of your face before your ancestors were born?" or "What is the sound of one hand clapping?" challenge one's usual way of relating to oneself and to the world. One may use logic to approach the koans, but real understanding transcends verbal explanations and depends on insight into one's ultimate nature.

The point of contemplating a koan isn't to get the right answer. Rather, it's to confront people with their preconceptions. Becoming frustrated because the usual intellect and emotions can't make sense of the koan, the sleeping mind will wake up. A koan can't be answered by the discursive superficial mind, but only by deep insight. Practitioners of the Rinzai tradition gain calm abiding by focusing the mind on the koan. They gain special insight by answering it.

When one finally breaks down a mental barrier and  suddenly penetrates into the meaning of reality, the resulting experience is called satori. A deep intuitive experience such as satori is not a goal in itself, but rather is a call to further practice. After a satori, one still needs to reveal one's Buddha nature even more. Although Zen talks about "sudden enlightenment," it seems like realizations are gained in a gradual manner. What is sudden is the collapsing of the last barrier in a series and the experience of new insight.

In daily life, Zen practitioners develop mindfulness in all actions, especially while working. Reflecting this, Ch'an monasteries in China altered one aspect of the vows of individual liberation and assigned Sangha members to manual labor such as agriculture. This originated from the needs of the monasteries to support themselves in ninth-century China. But, working can also be a tool for developing mindfulness and being attentive to all one does, says and thinks. While working mindfully, Zen practitioners cultivate the same inner silence experienced during sitting meditation. Work also reminds one that nirvana isn't to be sought elsewhere, but is actualized in the here and now.

Although Zen is a Mahayana tradition, many of its spiritual masters don't give extensive and explicit teachings on how to generate the altruistic intention. Instead they stress meditation and the arousal of wisdom. The idea behind this is that once the ego's preconceptions are cut and emptiness realized, the underlying unity of all people and things will become readily apparent. Then, compassion and love for others will naturally arise.

As the Zen tradition spread in East Asia, it put various cultural elements in its practice. For example, in Japan, flower arrangement, the tea ceremony, and gardening became ways to practice Zen in daily life. These activities also integrate into Buddhism the appreciation of nature and beauty found in Shinto, a pre-Buddhist religion in Japan.

The Japanese esteem the strict discipline of the warrior, so Zen practice emphasizes sitting in perfect meditative position and "conquering" the pain of an aching back and sore knees. Accordingly, in some monasteries, the meditation supervisor slaps slouching or sleeping meditators with a stick to awaken them.

Zen emphasizes simplicity in external appearances as well as in meditation practice. This was initially a reaction against the over-intellectualization of Chinese and Japanese scholars. In addition, many people were overwhelmed by the variety of Buddhist practices and sought an explicit and direct approach.

Nowadays, many people's homes and lives are often cluttered with the physical and mental paraphernalia of life in a technological society. The seeming simplicity of Zen appeals strongly to them. They enjoy entering an uncluttered meditation hall and appreciate the discipline of meditation. This is part of Zen's appeal to modern society.

# INTEGRATION OF SUTRA AND TANTRA:

*Tibetan Buddhism*

Buddhism was first brought to Tibet by two Buddhist princesses — one from Nepal, the other from China — who married the Tibetan king, Songtsen Gampo. But Buddhism wasn't widely established in Tibet until the eighth century, when the monk Santaraksita and the tantric yogi Padmasambhava came from India, bringing with them the Mahayana and Tantric teachings. In the eighth century, Ch'an Buddhism also went to Tibet from China.

Controversy soon arose among the Buddhist groups. Ch'an practitioners taught a kind of blank-minded meditation in which all conceptual thoughts, be they virtuous or not, were to be extinguished. Masters trained in the Indian tradition stressed first gaining a correct conceptual understanding and then going beyond that to direct experience in meditation. Ch'an asserted that realizations could come suddenly and spontaneously. Indian Buddhism stated that a gradual process, including good works as well as meditation, was necessary to become enlightened.

In India, debates were held to refute misconceptions of non-Buddhists and to enhance the Buddhists' understanding of the teachings. To settle the controversy, the Tibetan king proposed a debate, during which the Indian debater Kamalasila defeated the Chinese proponent of Ch'an. Since that time, Tibet has followed Indian Buddhism.

In the 11th century, several more lineages of teachings came to Tibet from India. These were called the New Translation Schools, in contrast to the Nyingma or Old Translation School of Padmasambhava. Among the New Translation schools were the Kadam, begun by the Indian monk and scholar Atisha, who taught widely in Tibet; the Sakya, founded by Drokmi, a Tibetan who went to Vikramasila University in India; and the Kargyu, started by Marpa, a Tibetan translator who practiced under the guidance of the great Indian master Naropa. The 14th century scholar and monk, Tzong Khapa drew from all the above lineages, but principally from the Kadam, and founded the Gelu tradition.

These Tibetan traditions are essentially the same, the principal difference being one of lineage. The basic meditations on the determination to be free, the altruistic intention and the wisdom realizing emptiness are similar in all the traditions.

Similarly, they all do certain preliminary practices. Nyingma, Kargyu and Sakya students often do the preliminaries during a three-year retreat, while Gelu students spread them out over a longer period of time. In Gelu, a three-year retreat is for more advanced practitioners who meditate continuously on a particular manifestation of the Buddha.

The Tibetan Buddhist traditions vary somewhat in their approach to the practice on the final stages of the tantric path and have different vocabulary to describe the meditation. But, as His Holiness the Dalai Lama, the religious and political leader of Tibet, repeatedly stresses, all of the traditions come to the same point and enlightenment can be attained through any of them.

The lineage of monks' and nuns' vows is the same in all Tibetan traditions. However, spiritual masters may be either ordained or lay. When they teach, some lay masters dress in maroon robes, similar to, but not exactly the same as, monks' and nuns' robes. Lay teachers often marry and have a family, but all monks and nuns in the Tibetan tradition take a vow of celibacy.

## Lama, Geshe and Rinpoche

People are often confused by Tibetan titles, which can be employed in a variety of ways. In the Gelu tradition, the title "lama," which may be translated as teacher, is generally given to respected masters. However, anyone who has disciples is technically a lama. In the other three traditions, "lama" is designated to any one who has completed a three-year meditation retreat. Thus, lamas may have very diverse abilities and training.

The title "geshe" is conferred on one who has undergone extensive philosophical training. It is like a Tibetan Ph.D. in Buddhist studies.

"Rinpoche" is a title meaning "precious" and is given in two circumstances. The predominant one is for the recognized reincarnation of a previous spiritual master. A less common usage is when disciples respectfully refer to their teacher as "Rinpoche."

The pre-Buddhist Bon religion in Tibet influenced some of the external forms that Buddhism took there, and it was, in turn, influenced greatly by Buddhism. The tradition of offering incense on mountain peaks came from Bon and was given a Buddhist meaning. So were prayer flags, brightly colored pieces of cloth strung on a line. Buddhist prayers and mantras are printed on them now, and the wind carries these good wishes throughout the world.

Much of the colorful and elaborate dancing expressing religious themes is also adapted from pre-Buddhist culture. The large drums, cymbals and horns are indigenous to Tibet, although the *vajra* (*dorje*), bell and small hand drum are tantric implements from India.

When importing Buddhism from India, Tibetans gave emphasis to accurate translations and standard technical terms. Teams of Indians and Tibetans translated as much of the Sanskrit canon from India as possible. As a result the Tibetan Canon is larger than the Chinese, although it doesn't contain all the Indian texts. The Chinese Canon has some texts not translated into Tibetan.

Many Indian commentaries on the sutras were translated into Tibetan, and the Tibetans soon added commentaries of their own. They imported the Indian system of debate and love for clear and concise explanation of the teachings, and this is apparent in Tibetan Buddhism today.

Tibetan Buddhism is found in the northern areas of modern India and in some areas in Nepal. In addition, it spread to Mongolia and Manchuria beginning in the 13th century. Since the Communist Chinese takeover of Tibet, which forced thousands of Tibetans to flee into exile in India and Nepal, Tibetan Buddhism is more accessible to others. Although Buddhism has been severely suppressed under the Communist Chinese government, Tibetan refugees have re-established monasteries in India. In addition, lamas and geshes have gone to many Western and Asian countries where Dharma centers have sprung up.

# Vajrayana

Tibetan Buddhism is a combination of both sutra — the Theravada and general Mahayana teachings — and tantra (Vajrayana or Mantrayana), which is a unique branch of the Mahayana. The Buddha taught the tantras to an audience of high bodhisattvas. These teachings weren't for public practice because they were suitable for the dispositions of only some people.

Thus, the tantric lineages were passed down privately from master to a few disciples in India. The Vajrayana practice became known more publicly starting in the sixth century. Although it spread throughout the Buddhist world, Vajrayana survived principally in Tibet and in the Japanese Shingon tradition.

Buddhist Tantra and Hindu Tantra should not be confused. Although the two have similar terminology and breathing exercises, they differ vastly in their philosophy, practice and results.

Tibetan masters stress that their students follow the teachings of all three traditions — Theravada, Mahayana and Vajrayana — all of which are found in Tibetan Buddhism. In the practice common with the Theravada, a practitioner takes refuge in the Triple Gem, observes ethical conduct, and develops the determination to be free. On this basis, one develops the altruistic intention to attain enlightenment for the benefit of all beings, which is the special emphasis of the Mahayana. One trains in the view of selflessness through the philosophical tenets of both the Theravada and Mahayana. Having developed to this extent, one then may take a tantric empowerment.

# Taking an Empowerment

An empowerment or initiation is conferred by a qualified spiritual master. In a specific ceremony, the teacher describes how to meditate and the disciple meditates at that time. Merely being present in the room or drinking consecrated water isn't sufficient to receive the empowerment. One must follow the instructions of the master and meditate. Some empowerments involve taking only the bodhisattva vows, while others require the tantric vows as well.

Some people believe that empowerments are given as blessings and that teachings on the determination to be free, the altruistic intention and the wisdom realizing emptiness (the three principals of the path) are advanced teachings. They think empowerment is some sort of magical blessing and crave to drink blessed water or be tapped on the head by sacred objects. This is not the correct understanding of Vajrayana.

The three principles of the path are basic teachings that all Buddhists should listen to and practice. They form the foundation and give people the motivation and understanding of the Dharma necessary to take empowerments.

Sometimes a master will give an empowerment in the form of a blessing so that people can form a karmic connection with the Vajrayana. Nevertheless, people must still concentrate at the time of the ceremony.

The purpose of an empowerment is to plant the seeds for future enlightenment and to introduce one to the meditation practice of a specific manifestation of the Buddha. Therefore, empowerments should be taken with a serious respectful attitude. Afterward, students should ask the master for instructions on the vows and commitments and then keep these as purely as possible.

In addition, students should request teachings on the actual practice — or sadhana — of that Buddha figure. The spiritual master will explain the philosophy of the Vajrayana and how to do the meditation of that Buddha figure or deity. By practicing according to instruction, one receives benefit.

Some people collect empowerments as if they were medals to pin on their coats. They boast to their friends how many holy masters have blessed them and how many empowerments they've received. But they don't do the daily meditation of these Buddha figures, nor are they mindful of what they do, say or think while they're at work and at home.

Such people won't advance in their practice for several reasons. First, their motivation is a worldly one — for prestige. A good motivation for practicing Dharma is to prepare for future rebirth, to attain liberation from cyclic existence or to become enlightened to be able to benefit others. True practitioners don't brag about their practice. As long as one isn't enlightened, there's nothing to boast about, and when one is enlightened, he or she is humble and doesn't brag.

Second, such people don't observe cause and effect in their daily lives, and thus continually create causes for unfortunate rebirths. To advance on the path, it's essential to live ethically and to be kind to others.

Third, they don't engage in the practice of the deities whose empowerments they received. Without putting effort into practice, there's no way to advance. Serious practitioners humbly follow the instructions given by their spiritual masters, and in this way attain realizations.

## Meditating on Buddhist Deities

We may wonder why Vajrayana deals with so many Buddha figures or deities. All Buddhas have the same realizations. However, for our benefit, they appear in a variety of physical forms in order to emphasize to us certain aspects of their realizations.

For example, Avalokiteshvara (Chenresig, Kuan Yin, Kannon) specifically shows compassion. One form of this Buddha figure has 1,000 arms, symbolizing continuously reaching out in a diversity of ways to help others. Another deity, Manjushri, is deep gold in color, representing the brilliance of wisdom. He is shown holding the sword of wisdom to illustrate the necessity of cutting through all obscurations to enlightenment. A female form of the Buddha, Tara, is green, which reminds us of the green of spring and summer, and thus represents prosperity, growth and success in the spiritual practice.

Some meditational deities are depicted embracing partners. This coming together of a male and a female deity is symbolic — it represents the union, attained in one's mind through meditation, of compassion (represented by the male figure) and wisdom (the female figure). This is artistic symbolism and in no way is license for unwise sexual behavior.

Tantric meditation involves working with the imagination. The mind has a tremendous capacity for visualization and imagination — in fact, these processes are involved when people become angry, attached or proud. In Vajrayana, this imaginative capacity of the mind is transformed and used in a positive way to approach enlightenment.

At the beginning of a tantric practice, one meditates on the emptiness or absence of any solid personal identity. From the spaciousness of emptiness, one imagines that the wisdom realizing emptiness manifests in the physical form of a Buddha figure, e.g. Avalokiteshvara. By simultaneously meditating on the appearance of oneself as Avalokiteshvara and the emptiness of inherent existence, a practitioner creates the causes to attain both the body and the mind of a Buddha.

Identification with Avalokiteshvara rouses the practitioner from feelings of inadequacy. By identifying with an ideal, the future Buddha one can become, a person adopts those characteristics and relates to others in a more loving and compassionate way now.

Recitation of mantras is done while imagining oneself in the pure form of a Buddha figure. A mantra is a prescribed set of syllables consecrated by a Buddha. It contains the essence of an enlightened being's realizations. Recitation of mantras can settle and concentrate the mind. In daily life, people chatter or hum in distraction. Reciting mantras transforms this already existing tendency into a beneficial practice leading to a focused and purified mental state.

In the Vajrayana, calm abiding is developed on the image of oneself as a Buddha, or on certain syllables or implements imagined at various points in the body. Special insight into emptiness is gained by focusing not only on the selflessness of oneself and the deity at the beginning of the meditation, but also on the emptiness of oneself as a Buddha during the meditation.

Tibetan Buddhism emphasizes the importance of finding a qualified spiritual master and then following his or her Dharma instructions properly. This is especially true for those doing the technical meditations of Vajrayana practice.

Tibetan Buddhism is spreading to Western countries. People are attracted by its step-by-step teachings to develop love, compassion and altruism, as well as its extensive and precise teachings to realize emptiness. Others are attracted by Vajrayana's use of imagination and transformation. But whatever tradition a person is inclined towards, it's important to be sincere, honest and humble in one's practice.

## Prominent Buddhist Traditions Existing Today

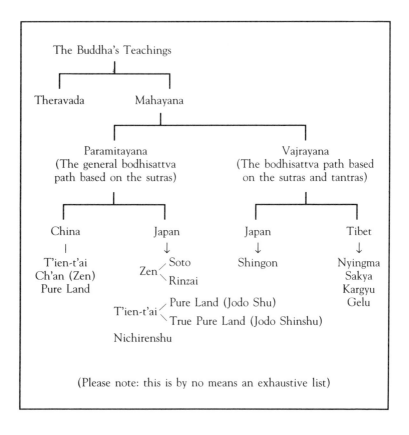

(Please note: this is by no means an exhaustive list)

WESTERN COUNTRIES

JAPAN

KOREA

TAIWAN

WESTERN COUNTRIES

CHINA

MONGOLIA

TIBET

NEPAL

DHARAMSALA

INDIA

BURMA

LAOS

VIETNAM

KAMP

THAILAND

WESTERN COUNTRIES

SUMATRA

INDONESIA

JAVA

SRI LANKA

WEST

AFGHANISTAN

PAKISTAN

WEST

IRAN

WEST

→ 6 B.C. – 1 B.C.
--→ 1 B.C. – 5 A.D.
-·-→ 5 A. D. – 15 A.D.
····→ 15 A.D. – 20 A.D.

157

When and Where Buddhism Spread

Buddhism was/is prevalent

Suppressed by communism

Lost to Islam

Lost to Hinduism

(times approximate)

158

# BUDDHIST TEMPLES AND
# DHARMA CENTERS:

*Places to come together*

The figure of the Buddha serenely sitting in meditation — this is the first thing we see upon entering a Buddhist temple. Our minds relax as we look at the peaceful figure, for we are finding that quiet and caring place inside ourselves. When we bow before a statue of the Buddha or place offerings on the shrine, we aren't propitiating an idol made of bronze; we're getting in touch with and respecting those parts in ourselves that resemble the Buddha.

A Buddhist temple is a place to remember the heights that human potential can attain. It's a place to recall that in spite of whatever disturbing emotions or problems we have in our lives, it's possible to transcend them. In the temple, we also remember that all beings — our friends, enemies and strangers — have the intrinsically pure Buddha nature. Our mood changes as we tap into these understandings.

Depending upon whether we have grown up in a Buddhist culture or not, many of the things in the temple may seem familiar or foreign to us. Also, each temple is slightly different according to which Buddhist tradition it follows.

In Theravada temples the figures of the Buddha are usually sitting in meditation, or reclining as when he passed away (the *parinirvana*). Often there is a bodhi tree in the courtyard, reminiscent of the bodhi under which Siddhartha attained enlightenment in Bodh Gaya. Outside the main temple, a four-faced statue is sometimes seen. Some people mistakenly call this the "four-faced Buddha," but actually it's a statue of four-faced Brahma, a Hindu deity which was part of Sri Lankan and Thai culture from pre-Buddhist times.

In Chinese temples, especially those of the Pure Land tradition, there are several Buddha figures. Included among these may be: the Medicine Buddha, showing the healing capacity of the Buddhas; Amitabha, reminding us of Sukhavati Pure Land where he presides; Avalokiteshvara (Kuan Yin), the manifestation of the compassion of all Buddhas; Manjushri on a lion, who embodies the wisdom of the

Buddhas; and Samantabhadra on an elephant, signifying the bodhisattva's practice and strong determination.

Although externally these Buddhas and bodhisattvas appear in different forms, as represented by the statues or paintings, they all have the same realizations of compassion, wisdom and so on. Because the realizations of Buddhas exist in their minds, which we can't perceive with our senses, they appear in forms that express their realizations and the special way in which they help others. Just as art expresses the thoughts and feelings of the artist in a physical form, the forms of the Buddhas symbolically express their realizations and ways of helping.

Chinese temples also may have fierce-looking bearded figures called Dharma protectors. Dharma protectors are either bodhisattvas or mundane deities who have pledged to protect the Dharma and its practitioners. The figures of the Dharma protectors remind us to protect the Dharma inside of us by practicing it purely, and not for worldly gain.

There is often a shrine in Chinese temples where the ancestral tablets of deceased relatives are placed. The names are written on red paper, as red is an auspicious color in Chinese culture. Relatives and friends place incense or fruit before the tablets, indicating their good wishes for the departed ones. The ancestral shrine isn't of Buddhist origin. It comes from Chinese culture.

Japanese temples, particularly those of the Zen tradition, have simple shrines, while Tibetan temples are generally elaborate. This reflects the cultures of the countries. Tibet, for instance, is a vast and sparsely-populated country of mountains and plateaus where one can see nothing for miles. It seems natural then, that the Tibetans would build colorful temples full of Buddha figures.

Some people erroneously say the forceful looking figures in Tibetan temples are demons. This is not the case at all. In line with the Vajrayana emphasis on transformation of ordinary emotions into divine wisdom, these figures represent wisdom and compassion demolishing self-grasping ignorance and selfishness, the roots of all our sufferings.

Buddhist devotees often bow or prostrate before the figures of the Buddhas and bodhisattvas in a temple. This is a sign of respect, not only to the beings who have become Buddhas and who thus have done what we want to do, but also to the future Buddhas that we'll become.

The candles, fruit, incense, water and so forth offered on the shrine also show our respect and admiration for Buddhahood. The Buddhas don't seek our prostrations or offerings: a fully enlightened one doesn't need an apple to be happy. Rather, making offerings is a way for us to train our minds to be joyful when giving. We offer because *we* need to: to develop spiritually, we must diminish our attachment and miserliness.

Almost anything can be offered on the shrine, as long as it was procured in ways that didn't harm others. Thus we shouldn't offer things obtained by overcharging customers. Nor should we offer meat, althjough in certain Vajrayana rituals, a small bit of meat is placed on the shrine and then mentally transformed through contemplating its lack of inherent existence. Flowers, lights, incense and water are the most common offerings. People can arrange them any way they consider beautiful and offer as much or as little as they wish.

Our motivation for offering is important. We shouldn't think we are "getting in good" with the Buddha so the Buddha will make us rich and powerful. First, holy beings can't be bribed. Second, we must create the cause to have happiness, and this comes through acting ethically and cultivating a kind heart.

Therefore before offering, it's advisable to cultivate the motivation to benefit others and to attain liberation or enlightenment. By offering, we'll create positive potential, which will bring not only temporary benefits, but also spiritual realizations.


## Activities at the Temples

Temples are centers of religious and cultural activities. People may come at any time to meditate or pray, and there are daily services which are chanted. The purpose of chanting is to guide our minds in a positive direction. By reflecting upon the meaning of what is being said, we can understand it better and integrate it in our hearts. Because we should contemplate while we chant, it's more appropriate to call this practice "chanted meditation."

The style of the services and chanting varies from one tradition to the next, depending on the culture of the country. Theravada services are chanted in Pali, while the Chinese, Vietnamese and Tibetans chant in their own languages. Now that Buddhism is coming to the West, we find a variety of languages used in Dharma centers, and Buddhism will certainly adapt its external forms and services to the cultures of Western countries.

Chanting is often done to the accompaniment of bells, gongs and drums. These are used to help the participants keep the melody of the chants, and also are an offering of music to the Buddhas.

Buddhist teachings and meditation classes are held at the temples. The importance of receiving Dharma teachings can't be stressed enough, for without learning we don't know how to practice properly.

In Asian cultures, some lay people take the Dharma for granted and are content simply to go to the temple, make offerings and participate in a chanting service, without doing any other practices. They feel that teachings are for monks and nuns, who have dedicated their lives to practicing the Dharma.

Happily, this is beginning to change, and more Asian lay people are interested in receiving extensive teachings. Teenagers and young adults are especially interested in learning the Dharma and practicing it during meditation sessions and in their daily lives. Asian Buddhists are now establishing Sunday schools for their children, rather than teaching them about Buddhism at home.

Western practitioners — be they monks, nuns or lay people — appreciate Dharma teachings very much, and will even travel great distances to obtain them. They go to the Dharma centers (Buddhist temples) especially to receive teachings and meditate, for they want to learn as well as to practice the teachings.

Some temples do social welfare projects such as setting up schools, youth groups, orphanages, clinics and old people's homes. His Holiness the Dalai Lama has encouraged more of these kinds of activities, for then we not only meditate on altruism, but also practice it.

For some people, social service is a very important part of their Dharma practice. For other people, study or meditation is foremost. Both lay followers and Sangha members can engage in all these activities, depending on their personal inclinations.

162

# BUDDHIST FESTIVALS AND RITES:

*Holidays, birth, marriage and death*

Buddhism follows the lunar calendar, so full and new moon days are times of special activities. Many lay followers go to the temples to participate in chanting services, pray, and create positive potential by making offerings. Some take the eight precepts for the day. Many Chinese temples offer vegetarian lunch to the public on those days.

The full and new moon days also mark the purification and confession days of the monks and nuns. They recite and review their vows, and renew their determination to keep them purely in the future.

The most important Buddhist holiday is Vesak, the day the Buddha became enlightened. This is celebrated on the 15th day of the fourth month in the lunar calendar, which usually falls in May or June. People often take the eight precepts on this day, and flock to the temples to participate in services.

Some traditions say Vesak is also the day of the Buddha's birth and passing away, while others celebrate the Buddha's birthday on the eighth day of the fourth lunar month. On this day, Buddhists of some traditions will symbolically wash a statue of the Buddha with scented water to recall the gods bathing the Buddha after he was born.

Seven weeks after Vesak is the anniversary of the Buddha's first teaching — also called the Turning of the Dharma Wheel. This marks the time when the Buddha taught the Four Noble Truths in Sarnath.

Tibetan Buddhists distinguish four special days in the Buddha's life, the first two being Vesak and the Turning of the Dharma Wheel. On the 15th day of the first lunar month, they celebrate the day that the Buddha demonstrated miraculous powers to non-believers, resulting in their following the Buddhist path. The fourth holiday is celebrated a week after the end of the rainy season retreat. This marks the Buddha's return to our world after having gone to a god-realm for three months to teach his mother the Dharma.

The yearly rainy season retreat, lasting for three months during the summer, has been observed by monks and nuns since the time of the Buddha. In India, many insects and animals multiply during the summer monsoon rains. To prevent their accidental deaths, the Buddha had his followers stay in a specific area during this time, instead of moving from one locality to the other.

This is a time of retreat for the Sangha, during which they aren't allowed to accept robes, bedding and so forth. A special ceremony marks the end of the rainy season retreat. This is followed by the *kathina* ceremony, in which the laity offers new robes to the Sangha, for at the end of the monsoons their possessions are worn out by the dampness.

In Chinese Buddhism, the anniversaries of various bodhisattvas are celebrated. These days mark occasions referred to in the scriptures when bodhisattvas were born, first generated the altruistic intention, or made special vows to help others.

As Buddhism spread to many cultures, it conformed to the cultural activities of those places. As a result, some cultural activities continued as before, only were now given a Buddhist flavor. One example is Lunar New Year, a holiday observed by many pre-Buddhist cultures. In Tibet, Buddhist prayer services were added to the general celebration and elaborate offerings to the Buddhas, bodhisattvas and Dharma protectors were made.

In addition, the Great Prayer Festival was begun in Lhasa in the early 14th century, attracting Sangha and lay people from all over Tibet. His Holiness the Dalai Lama or other great practitioners would teach during this time, and candidates for the Geshe degree would debate. Unfortunately, the communists occupying Tibet have virtually stifled the Great Prayer Festival, but the Tibetans in exile continue to celebrate it.

## Marriage, Birth and Death

There is no formal "baptism" ceremony for children born in Buddhist families. However, parents may make offerings and prayers and request chanted meditations for the benefit of their newborn child. When children are old enough to understand the Dharma, they may take refuge and "officially" become Buddhists.

In Buddhism, marriage is considered a secular matter. In fact, the

Buddha prohibited monks and nuns from match-making or performing marriage ceremonies. This is to help them to preserve their celibacy vow and to avoid taking time from study and meditation.

Sometimes lay Buddhists perform marriages, including discussion of Buddhist beliefs in the ceremony. Or, after a secular ceremony Buddhist couples go to the temple, make offerings or sponsor a prayer session to create positive potential for a happy marriage. At this time monks and nuns perform chanted meditations and pray for the couple's lives to be happy and beneficial for themselves and others.

During times of difficulty, people often request the Sangha to recite the sutras, do chanted meditations (*puja*) and pray for them. However, Buddhists don't pray to the Buddha as an all-powerful God and ask him to solve their problems. Buddhists believe that no one, even the Buddha, is omnipotent. If someone were all-powerful, he or she surely would have eliminated the world's problems by now.

Nor must we ask the Buddha to have mercy on us and cease punishing us for our harmful deeds. Buddhas have infinite compassion and never inflict harm on others, even in the name of "justice." Our suffering is due to our own destructive actions done in this or previous lives.

Reading sutras, performing chanted meditations and making offerings in times of distress are done for two reasons. First they purify the imprints of our destructive actions, so they won't ripen in the future. In addition, they create positive potential which will bring happiness as its result. Sometimes these ceremonies are held in the homes of the devotees, while other times they are held in the temple or monastery.

When people die, the Sangha is often requested to do chanted meditations for the benefit of the deceased. Some of the chanted texts may be instructions to the dying or dead person, to help him or her have a good rebirth. Others accumulate positive potential which is then dedicated to all beings, but especially for the benefit of the dying or dead.

Although in Asian cultures, the monks and nuns are usually asked to conduct these ceremonies, lay followers may also do them. In Western Dharma centers, lay followers and Sangha generally perform them together. People shouldn't have the attitude "I'm a lay person so

I can't do chanted meditations." Nor should they think they're hiring the Sangha to do it for them, while they relax. When we have close connections with others, it's extremely beneficial if we pray, read Dharma texts, make offerings and do chanted meditations for their benefit.

Buddhist festivals are many and varied. What has been explained here is only a limited sample. Feel free to visit Buddhist temples, monasteries or Dharma centers on festival days. Ask practitioners about the significance of the ceremonies and holidays. Also, when you visit temples, you needn't engage in practices you don't understand — bowing, for example. The spirit of Buddhism is one of free inquiry and understanding. Let's take advantage of this openness to learn.

# IV

# BUDDHISM TODAY

*Buddhism in the 20th century faces two challenges. The first is to clarify misconceptions people have about it. Some people confuse Buddhism with ancestor worship, others with fortune telling. These issues need to be clarified for us to properly understand the Buddha's teachings.*

*In addition, religious harmony is essential for world peace. Buddhism is renowned for its tolerance and appreciation of other religions, yet Buddhists remain firm on their own path. How does this remarkable attitude come about?*

# WHAT IS BUDDHISM,
# WHAT IS SUPERSTITION?:

*What Buddhism says about ghosts, fortune-telling and psychic powers*

The Buddha's teachings deal with mental development. The real path to enlightenment unfolds within a person's mind. While this path can't be altered according to time and place, the external forms that Buddhism takes vary from country to country as rites and rituals are integrated with the cultural forms of each place.

Sometimes the integration of Buddhism with native cultures has led to a lack of clear distinction between Buddhist and non-Buddhist practices. Although the Sangha know the difference between native traditions and Buddhist practices and maintain a high standard in Buddhist practice, in the lives of many lay people, these are mixed.

For example, some people consider themselves Buddhists and have a statue of the Buddha flanked by Chinese gods in their temple. They are unclear about the difference between the Buddhas and bodhisattvas and the native worldly gods, and thus pray to all of them equally. Some of the practices performed in these temples — going into trance, fortune-telling and so on — are not Buddhist practices. They are folk customs, popularized Taoism, or ancestor worship.

## Helping Deceased Relatives

One example of people thinking a practice of ancestor worship is Buddhism is the burning of paper goods and money for deceased relatives. Folk culture believes that after death, everyone is reborn in a spirit nether world similar to our human world with houses, clothes, credit cards and so forth. Living family members wish to demonstrate filial piety and provide for their deceased relatives. They also want to prevent neglected spirits from harming them. To do this, they burn paper houses, clothes, etc. to offer them to their deceased relatives. They believe this transfers the goods to the nether world where their deceased relatives enjoy them.

Burning paper goods is ancestor worship, not Buddhism. According to Buddhism, people aren't born in a spirit nether world after death. Instead, they enter an intermediate state before being reborn in another body. The intermediate state may be as short as one moment or as long as 49 days, after which they are definitely reborn. Intermediate state beings do not have the ability to communicate with us, nor we with them. Only other intermediate state beings and people with clairvoyance attained through meditation can perceive intermediate state beings.

After the intermediate state, people are reborn in one of the six realms of cyclic existence — god, demi-god, human, animal, hungry ghost and hellish being. While some beings are reborn as spirits, who are included in the hungry ghost realm, not everyone is. Rebirth in any realm is temporary, not eternal, and people's previous actions or karma influence what they are reborn as.

Our deceased relatives will have possessions according to the realm they are born in. For example, if Grandma died one year ago, by now she would have been reborn in another realm. If she was reborn as a human, by now she would be a tiny baby. She (or maybe he, because we may change sex from one lifetime to the next) would have food and shelter provided by her new parents. Burning paper dresses doesn't give Grandma new baby clothes.

Although it's natural to miss our loved ones when they die, trying to contact them through mediums isn't beneficial. The Buddha's first teaching was about the transience of life. Our minds will be more peaceful if we accept the death of our loved ones.

It's good to want to help departed relatives and friends, and there are Buddhist practices to do this. We can offer the deceased's possessions to charities or to religious institutions and practitioners. Also, we can do special prayers and practices or request the Sangha to do them, and dedicate the positive potential for the deceased ones.

We can't transfer our good karma to others like transferring money from one bank account to another, for the person who does the action is the one who experiences the karmic result. However, by dedicating our positive potential for the well-being of deceased ones, we create conducive circumstances whereby their previously created good karma can ripen. The good karmic imprints on their mindstreams are like seeds in a field. Our prayers and dedication of positive potential resemble the water and fertilizer which make the seeds grow.

The best way to help our parents have a good rebirth is to encourage them to act positively and stop acting destructively while they're alive. Thus, we should encourage our family to be generous and patient with others. We shouldn't ask them to lie on our behalf or to deceive others to get more money for the family. In this way, they'll have many good karmic imprints and few bad ones to carry with them to future lives.

## The Festival of the Seventh Month and Ullambana

The Festival of the Seventh Month is particularly confusing for many Asians. This is a non-Buddhist holiday for those practicing ancestor worship. It is often confused with the Buddhist holiday of Ullambana, celebrated on the 15th day of the same month. The mix-up between the two arose because both festivals occur during the seventh lunar month and both are done to benefit deceased relatives. However, the philosophy and practice of the two are quite different.

In ancestor worship one sets out food and incense offerings to ancestral tablets or to effigies of deceased relatives in the seventh lunar month. Also, paper money, houses and so forth are burned in the hope that the dead will receive and enjoy them. According to folk belief, the beings in the hellish realm are released for a month and roam the earth. To provide for their needs, and to win their favor and prevent them from harming the living, relatives make offerings to them.

However, as explained above, not everyone is reborn as a spirit and burned goods don't reach them. Also, spirits belong to the hungry ghost realm and don't live in the hellish realm. Also, according to Buddhism, those who are temporarily born in unfortunate states such as the hellish realms don't have a holiday in the seventh month during which they roam around our world.

The Buddhist festival of Ullambana falls on the 15th day of the seventh month. It stems from the *Ullambana Sutra*, found in the

Chinese Buddhist Canon (it isn't found in the Tibetan or Pali Canons). This sutra tells the story of Maudgalyayana, one of the Buddha's foremost disciples, who by means of clairvoyance saw that his mother had been reborn as a hungry ghost. He lovingly brought her some food, which she hid because she was too miserly to share it with others. When she later took it out, it was rotten. Saddened, Maudgalyayana wanted to help his mother's plight, but didn't know how.

He asked advice from the Buddha, who recommended he make offerings of food and other necessities to the assembly of Sangha, request them to meditate, and dedicate the positive potentials created by both himself and the Sangha for his mother's benefit. Maudgalyayana did this on the 15th day of the seventh month. The resultant positive potential helped his mother's own previously created positive potential (good karma) to ripen. Her life as a hungry ghost ended and she was reborn in more fortunate circumstances.

Thus, many Chinese and Japanese Buddhists celebrate Ullambana by offering to the Sangha, requesting them to do prayers and meditation, and dedicating the positive potential for the benefit of departed relatives and friends. Thus, we can see Ullambana is different in content and philosophy from the non-Buddhist Festival of the Seventh Month.

## Spirits and Gods

According to Buddhism, some people may be temporarily reborn as spirits due to the actions they did in the past. Among the six realms, spirits are one type of hungry ghost. Sometimes, people are born in the god (*deva*) realm. Both spirits and gods can speak through mediums.

Generally, when a medium goes into trance, his or her consciousness is temporarily suppressed and a spirit or god speaks through the medium's body. Spirits may be helpful or harmful, just as human beings may help or harm us. Spirits and gods are worldly beings, subject to birth and death in cyclic existence. They lack the perfect wisdom and compassion of the Buddhas. Some spirits and gods have limited clairvoyant powers. Thus, sometimes their predictions are accurate, but other times they aren't. They may identify themselves as a deceased relative or as a bodhisattva, but that doesn't mean they actually are telling the truth.

The practice of spirits and gods speaking through mediums is folk culture. The Buddha did not teach this. He taught the path to enlightenment and encouraged us to develop our own wisdom to make decisions. We should always reflect if the action we're going to do is ethical or not. Is it motivated by genuine loving-kindness or by anger, attachment or closed-mindedness?

Many people fear being harmed by spirits. Spirits can harm humans only when a person has created the cause to be harmed — i.e. if he or she has harmed others in this or previous lives. There is no benefit in fearing spirits. In fact fear and paranoia open the door to receiving harm from spirits. Even if a real spirit doesn't harm, a fearful person's mind will create an imaginary spirit that does.

Dreaming about the deceased doesn't mean they have returned. This is most likely a product of our imagination. When we dream of an apple, it isn't a real apple. Likewise, when we dream about a dead relative, it isn't that person.

When people are afraid of spirits or are being harmed by them, refuge and compassion are the best antidotes. If we imagine the Buddha and take strong refuge in the Buddhas, Dharma and Sangha, spirits can't harm us and the fear soon disappears.

Spirits are sentient beings just like human beings. They want to be happy and not have suffering, just like we do. Understanding this, we can feel compassion for them and wish them to be free from all misery. On one hand, loving-kindness prevents us from being fearful: we're more concerned with others — in this case the spirit — than with ourselves. On the other hand, just as most people don't intentionally harm someone who has compassion for them, spirits won't harm someone who wishes them well.

In conclusion, it's wiser for us to practice the Buddha's teachings as explained in the four noble truths and the gradual path to enlightenment, than to get involved with worldly spirits. Like other sentient beings, spirits should be objects of our compassion.

# Geomancy and Fortune-telling

Geomancy, the positioning of buildings, furniture, graves and so forth to bring good fortune and prosperity, is an art developed in East Asian cultures. It isn't part of Buddhism, although some Chinese Buddhist monks practice it. Buddhist monks may play chess, but that doesn't mean chess is Buddhism. Geomancy is similar: it comes from the general culture of a country.

Some Buddhists — and non-Buddhists too — consult fortune-tellers. However, that doesn't mean fortune-telling is Buddhism. Although some people like to consult fortune-tellers, it's unwise to over-emphasize their predictions. To paraphrase His Holiness the Dalai Lama, "We never know the future until it happens."

Asking Buddhist monks or nuns to give a lottery-winning number is inappropriate. Spinning wheels in front of a Buddha statue to get a lucky number is similarly incorrect, especially since the Buddha discouraged people from wasting their money on gambling.

# Clairvoyance

Some people are fascinated by supernatural powers and seek them as the goal of spiritual practice. However, the aim of practicing Dharma isn't to attain clairvoyance, it's to receive enlightenment for the benefit of others.

Ordinary clairvoyance can came from a variety of causes. It may be due to karma — previous lives' actions and prayers. This clairvoyance isn't always reliable and is lost at death.

True and reliable clairvoyance is attained through meditative concentration. Here, clairvoyance comes as a by-product of meditation, just as when one buys rice, the bag comes along with it. One needn't cultivate clairvoyance separately.

A person's motivation determines whether or not their psychic powers are beneficial. Those who seek reputation and material offerings as a result of having psychic powers have worldly motivations. Those who are proud and boast about their clairvoyance risk using it to enhance their egos rather than subdue them. They may misuse their powers, causing suffering for themselves and others. For these reasons, an impartial loving and compassionate attitude towards all beings is essential to use psychic powers wisely.

The Buddha forbade his disciples to brag about their attainments or to use their supernatural abilities flamboyantly. True spiritual practitioners are humble. They prefer to quietly serve others rather than to draw attention and admiration to themselves.

Having clairvoyance isn't special. All of us have had it in previous lives. But it hasn't done us much good for we're still taking rebirth in cyclic existence due to the force of our disturbing attitudes and karma.

Practicing the path to enlightenment, however, brings lasting benefit for ourselves and others. Therefore, we should use the great opportunity we have in this lifetime to study and practice the Dharma. The best "magical power" is a kind heart and a sense of universal responsibility caring for the welfare of all beings. These qualities are more rare and valuable than clairvoyant powers.

If we are sincerely interested in attaining enlightenment for the benefit of all beings, then it's essential to be able to discriminate the path described by the Buddha from cultural customs, superstition and wrong paths. To do this, we should listen to teachings from qualified masters, and then examine them carefully and ask questions to clarify our doubts. By practicing the correct path, we'll be able to attain enlightenment.

# RELIGIOUS HARMONY

*Diversity is beneficial*

The teachings I heard at my first meditation course deeply changed my life. What impressed me wasn't that they were Buddhist teachings, but that they made sense. I didn't care who spoke them or what the name of the religion was, because my real interest was in the meaning of the teachings and their significance in my daily life.

At that time, I didn't know the terms Mahayana and Theravada, nor did I care. I didn't understand the words Nyingma, Kargyu, Gelu and Sakya. Zen, Pure Land, Vajrayana were just names to me. To this day, I feel uncomfortable when people ask which Buddhist tradition I follow, for in my heart I'm simply another human being seeking the path to happiness and a way to make my life meaningful to others.

Labels too often divide people. Instead of understanding the real meaning and purpose of something, we're attached to the name. We judge and discriminate others on the basis of the labels attached to them, rather than try to understand who they really are or what they really believe. We create a general conception of what a certain name means, and then assume everyone who has that label is alike. Our limited minds think, "If you're a Theravada, you don't listen to Mahayana teachings. If you're a Christian, you're not a Buddhist. If you're religious, you're not scientific."

On the basis of thinking, "I'm a 'this' and they're a 'that'," we argue. This happens amongst Buddhists and between Buddhists and those of other religions. Fortunately, no wars have ever been fought in the name of the Buddha or in order to protect or spread Buddhism. Nevertheless, any kind of closed-minded sectarian attitude is harmful, for it not only impedes our own spiritual progress, it also causes friction among people.

How does sectarianism harm our own progress? In Buddhism, the two chief qualities we want to develop are wisdom and compassion. If we're attached to our own religion, we take it as a personal affront when someone disagrees with what we believe. Becoming angry and aggressive, we defend our beliefs and attack others'. At this point, we stop seeking the truth and start defending our religion simply because it's ours.

Such angry closed-mindedness leaves negative karmic imprints on our mindstreams. Obscuring our minds, these imprints prevent us from gaining wisdom. In addition, anger is totally opposite to compassion, the wish for all others to be free from suffering. Thus, sectarianism hinders our development of wisdom and compassion, and leads us further from enlightenment rather than toward it.


## Harmony Among Buddhist Traditions

Having a general overview of the path to enlightenment enables us to understand that all teachings given by the Buddha are advice he gave to students about how to practice at different stages of their development. None of the teachings are to be abandoned, neglected or criticized for they all are suitable to be practiced at some level of our development. If we criticize the Buddha's teachings and thus neglect to test and practice them, we're abandoning the very methods that can lead us to realizations.

This doesn't mean, however, that we need to practice all the teachings at this very moment. What the Buddha taught is vast and profound, and we have to approach it gradually. We should practice whatever corresponds to our dispositions and whatever we're capable of at the present. There is no pressure to do everything immediately. Slowly, we'll evolve and can integrate more and more teachings into our practice. Temporarily leaving aside some of the teachings because they're beyond our scope is different from criticizing them.

People have the tendency to want to be best. But what does "best" mean? Children's books are best for children and adult books are best for adults. We can't say that either children's or adults' books are best. Similarly, it's best for someone to read English books if that's the only language he or she knows, but for a Chinese speaking person, Chinese literature is best. There is no absolute "best" that applies to everyone.

The essential point is to realize that not everyone is alike. We may like one food and someone else may like another, but both nourish and sustain life. Likewise, one person may be attracted to the Theravada tradition and another to the Mahayana, but both enable people to improve themselves and to progress on the path. This applies also to people who follow Buddhism and those who don't. As long as a philosophy encourages people to avoid harming others and to help them as much as possible, it's beneficial.

We should avoid criticizing other Buddhist traditions because their ways of practice are different from ours. For example, some people are inspired by devotion, ritual and prayer. Other people don't find these appealing, and prefer silent meditation instead. We aren't all alike, nor should we be. It's wonderful that so many Buddhist traditions exist, so we each can find one that suits our personality and helps us to develop.

Similarly, we shouldn't criticize any of the Buddha's teachings if we feel they don't fit us. The Buddha gave teachings that corresponded to the mentality of his audience. For example, the Buddha taught different views of selflessness according to the audience he was speaking to. From this, four main philosophical schools arose, each based on different sutras and each with its own assertion of the meaning of selflessness.

It's unwise for us to disdain any of these views or schools, for they are suitable for certain groups of people, at particular levels of development. Nor should we be proud and think, "I study the highest view. There's no need for me to learn the others." In fact, the great masters say we can't understand the final view of selflessness, unless we have previously understood those of the other schools.

The diversity of philosophical assertions is stimulating. It makes us wonder, "Which is the final view? How do things really exist?" To answer this, we have to learn and examine all views. In this way our wisdom increases. Realizing emptiness isn't a matter of repeating by rote a certain dogma. It depends on understanding, and this comes through thinking about the various philosophical views.

Nor should we criticize other traditions when they use a term differently from the way we do. One word may have different meanings in various traditions. If we forget this fact, we may read a book from another tradition and impose our definitions onto certain words, distorting their meaning in that context. Then of course those teachings don't make sense to us. However, if we have vast learning, then we'll understand the meaning of the terms correctly and will see that the various traditions come to the same point.

Referring to the difference in vocabulary used by the four Tibetan Buddhist traditions to describe the final stage of the practice, His Holiness the Dalai Lama said in *Kindness, Clarity and Insight*, "Transcending sectarianism, we can find much to evoke deep realization by seeing how these schools come down to the same basic thought."

Both the bodhisattva vows and the tantric vows contain injunctions against disparaging any of the Buddha's teachings. *The Sutra of an All-inclusive Interweaving of Everything*, states:

> O Manjushri, to regard some of the enlightening words spoken by the tathagata (Buddha) as good and some as bad is to discard the Dharma. To say this is reasonable while that is not...(or) this was spoken (only) for the sake of bodhisattvas, and that was spoken (only) for hearers...(or) this is something in which bodhisattvas need not train is to discard the Dharma.

## Buddhism and Other Religions

The great leaders of all the world's religions have sought to benefit others by sharing with them their own spiritual experiences. However, common people have become attached to the names of those experiences and philosophies, and fought with those who didn't agree or whose faith had a different name. The number of people who have been killed in the name of religion throughout history is appalling. None of the founders of the world's great religions would be pleased by the amount of blood that has been shed in their names.

The great holy beings aren't attached to labels because they seek meaning, harmony and love. They have no need to prove they are right and theirs is the only way. Most of the great religious leaders have lived simply and have found happiness inside themselves. They haven't sought praise, wealth, power and glory. Hostile sectarianism and religious prejudice isn't the way of the holy people of any religion, for they want their followers to live in peace with all other beings.

All religions share certain crucial points. They recognize that material development alone isn't the path to happiness, and that a greater happiness than that received through our senses exists. All religions strive to help humans improve themselves by developing patience, love and respect for each other. They want people to cultivate good attitudes toward one another and then to implement these in service to the larger community. To this end, all faiths propound ethical values to help us regulate our behavior. In *Kindness, Clarity and Insight*, His Holiness the Dalai Lama says:

> The motivation of all religious practice is similar — love, sincerity, honesty. The way of life of practically all religious persons is contentment. The teachings of tolerance, love and compassion are the same. A basic goal is the benefit of humankind — each type of system seeking in its own unique ways to improve human beings. If we put too much emphasis on our philosophy, religion, or theory, are too attached to it, and try to impose it on other people, it makes trouble. Basically all the great teachers, such as Gautama Buddha, Jesus Christ, or Mohammed, founded their new teachings with a motivation of helping their fellow humans. They did not mean to gain anything for themselves nor to create more trouble or unrest in the world.

Being a Buddhist doesn't mean bowing to the Buddha, chanting Buddhist prayers or having a shrine with a statue of the Buddha. The essence of Buddhism is wisdom and compassion, and these can be expressed and shared with others without any Buddhist terminology. Similarly, the essence of Christian, Hindu, Jewish and Islamic teachings is ethics and love. These qualities are universal.

In terms of philosophy, there are differences — some religions believe in a creator God, while others, like Buddhism, do not. It is naive to say all religious philosophies are the same. Perhaps from the viewpoint of those who have realized and experienced them, they are. It could be that the mystical experiences of holy beings of all religions are same, but the expressions of these in terms and concepts is different. Words are limiting, they are facsimiles of reality. Thus, the experience may be the same, but the words describing it different.

However, for us ordinary beings, concepts point the direction to the experience. Thus we must analyze the various philosophies and determine which one best enables us to purify our minds and develop our good qualities. There is no need to criticize others because different philosophies appeal to them. Although we may discuss and debate philosophy together, pointing out inconsistencies in one and virtues of another, this doesn't mean we put down the people who believe them.

From a Buddhist point of view, the diversity of philosophies is beneficial, for not everyone sees things in the same way. We're all at different levels, we have different interests and inclinations. Therefore, it's beneficial for a wide range of religions to exist so everyone can find something suitable for his or her character. It would be terrible if we all had to fit into one mold and think in exactly the same way. Also, that would be impossible. His Holiness the Dalai Lama said,

> I think that differences in faith are useful. There is a richness in the fact that there are so many different presentations of the way. Given that there are so many different types of people with various predispositions and inclinations, this is helpful.

## Inter-religious Dialogue

In Europe, North America and Australia, inter-religious dialogue is increasing. When the Dalai Lama goes to Europe, he is hosted by the Vatican. One high official in the Episcopalian Church introduced His Holiness when he spoke at Westminster Abbey in 1985. Some Tibetan monks and nuns have visited Catholic monasteries in America and some American Catholic monks and nuns have stayed in Japanese Buddhist temples. Within Buddhism, there are international conferences and seminars attended by representatives of all Buddhist traditions. These are just a few instances, there are many more.

Although it's essential for world peace that today's great religious leaders meet and learn from each other, it's equally important for common practitioners to do so as well. Not only does inter-religious dialogue enable us to pray and meditate together and thus share our internal peace, it also helps to prevent superstition, misconception and fear of other religious groups.

Personally, I've benefited greatly from discussions with people of other faiths. I understand better how the human mind works and how to communicate with people in ways that they understand. My mind becomes more flexible and can go beyond the words people are using to the meanings they're expressing. I've also received some excellent guidance as well: when a Catholic nun who had been ordained over 50 years ago told me of the various stages of development she experienced on her religious journey and the obstacles she had to overcome, I saw many parallels with Buddhist practice. This gave me, a younger nun, courage to go through the difficult times in the practice.

Once I spoke with a female Baptist minister, and we compared our experiences as women in religion. This was very rewarding and stimulating. Speaking with a Jewish rabbi, I was astonished to learn that some ancient Jewish worship practices resembled Buddhist ones. When reading a book on Christian contemplation, I noticed it was similar to the "guru yoga" practice in Tibetan Buddhism. These experiences have helped me to appreciate both the diversity and the unity in human religious thought.

Appreciating others' religions and beliefs doesn't jeopardize our commitment to our own. Rather, as we look beyond the words to their meaning, as we look beyond superficial differences to a common aim, our wisdom and compassion will grow, and our own faith in the Three Jewels will increase.

# GLOSSARY

**Altruistic intention (bodhicitta)** — the mind dedicated to attaining enlightenment in order to benefit all others.

**Arhat** — a person who has attained liberation and is thus free from cyclic existence.

*Bhikshu, Bhikshuni* — a fully-ordained monk or nun, respectively.

**Bodhisattva** — a person who has developed the spontaneous altruistic intention.

**Buddha** — any person who has purified all defilements and developed all good qualities. "The Buddha" refers to Shakyamuni Buddha, who lived 2,500 years ago in India.

**Buddha figure** — a manifestation of the Buddha, a Buddhist deity.

**Buddha nature (Buddha potential)** — the innate qualities of the mind enabling all beings to attain enlightenment.

**Calm abiding** — the ability to remain single-pointedly on the object of meditation with a pliant and blissful mind.

**Cessation** — the absence of an obscuration — for example, anger — so that it can never arise again. When all disturbing attitudes have been eliminated, we attain nirvana.

**Compassion** — the wish for all others to be free from suffering and its causes.

**Cyclic existence** — uncontrollably being reborn under the influence of disturbing attitudes and karmic imprints.

**Deluded obscurations** — disturbing thoughts and karma that cause rebirth in cyclic existence. When the deluded obscurations are removed, one becomes an arhat.

**Dependent arising** — the fact that all phenomena are dependent on parts and on the mind which conceives and labels them. Many phenomena — our body, tables, etc. — also depend on causes and conditions to exist.

**Determination to be free** — the attitude aspiring to be free from all problems and sufferings and to attain liberation.

**Dharma** — our wisdom realizing emptiness and the absence of suffering and its causes that this wisdom brings. In a more general sense, Dharma refers to the teachings and doctrine of the Buddha.

**Disturbing attitudes** — attitudes such as ignorance, attachment, anger, pride, jealousy and closed-mindedness, which disturb our mental peace and propel us to act in ways harmful to others.

**Empowerment** — a ceremony in Vajrayana Buddhism in which the disciple is authorized to meditate on a particular manifestation of the Buddha.

**Emptiness** — the lack of independent or inherent existence. This is the ultimate nature or reality of all persons and phenomena.

**Enlightenment (Buddhahood)** — the state of a Buddha, i.e. the state of having forever eliminated all obscurations from our mindstream, and having developed our good qualities and wisdom to their fullest extent. Buddhahood supersedes liberation.

**Hearers** — followers of the Buddha who aspire to become arhats. They are so called because they hear the Buddha's doctrine and then teach it to others.

**Imprint** — the residual energy left on the mindstream when an action has been completed. When it matures, it influences our experience.

**Impute** — to give a label or name to an object. To give meaning to an object.

**Inherent or independent existence** — a false and non-existent quality that we project onto persons and phenomena; existence independent of causes and conditions, parts or the mind labeling a phenomenon.

**Initiation** — see empowerment.

**Karma** — intentional action. Our actions leave imprints on our mindstreams which bring about our experiences.

**Liberation** — freedom from cyclic existence.

**Love** — the wish for all others to have happiness and its causes.

**Mahayana** — the Buddhist tradition that asserts all beings can attain enlightenment. It strongly emphasizes the development of compassion and the altruistic intention.

**Mantra** — a series of syllables consecrated by a Buddha and expressing the essence of the entire path to enlightenment. They are recited to concentrate and purify the mind.

**Meditation** — habituating ourselves with positive attitudes and correct perspectives.

**Mind** — the experiential, cognitive part of living beings. Non-physical, the mind isn't made of atoms, nor is it perceivable through our five senses.

**Mindstream** — the continuity of the mind.

**Nirvana** — the cessation of suffering and its causes.

**Obscurations to all-knowing** — stains of the disturbing attitudes that prevent perceiving all existent phenomena. When both the deluded obscurations and the obscurations to all-knowing are removed, we become a fully-enlightened Buddha.

**Positive potential** — imprints of positive actions, which will result in happiness in the future. Sometimes translated as "merit" or "good karma."

**Pure Land** — a Mahayana Buddhist tradition emphasizing methods to be reborn in a pure land. A pure land is a place established by a Buddha or bodhisattva where all conditions are conducive for the practice of Dharma and the attainment enlightenment.

**Realization** — a clear, deep and correct understanding of what the Buddha taught. This may be either conceptual or non-conceptual, direct experience. The non-conceptual direct realizations gained at higher levels of the path cleanse the obscurations from our minds forever.

*Samsara* — cyclic existence

**Sangha** — any person who directly and non-conceptually realizes emptiness. In a more general sense, Sangha refers to the communities of ordained monks and nuns. It sometimes is used to refer to Buddhists in general.

**Selflessness** — see emptiness.

**Solitary Realizers** — followers of the Buddha who aspire for arhatship and who attain nirvana during times when a Buddha hasn't appeared in the world.

**Special insight (*vipassana*)** — a wisdom thoroughly discriminating phenomena. It is conjoined with calm abiding and enables us to analyze the meditation object and simultaneously remain single-pointedly on it. This removes ignorance.

**Suffering (*dukkha*)** — any dissatisfactory condition. It doesn't refer only to physical or mental pain, but includes all problematic and unsatisfactory conditions.

**Sutra** — a scripture containing a teaching of the Buddha. Sutras are found in all Buddhist traditions.

**Taking refuge** — entrusting our spiritual development to the guidance of the Buddhas, Dharma and Sangha.

**Tantra** — a scripture describing the Vajrayana practice. This term can also refer to the Vajrayana practice.

**Theravada** — the Tradition of the Elders. A Buddhist tradition popular in Southeast Asia and Sri Lanka.

**Three Jewels** — the Buddhas, Dharma and Sangha.

**Vajrayana** — a Mahayana Buddhist tradition popular in Tibet and Japan.

**Wisdom realizing reality (wisdom realizing emptiness)** — an attitude which correctly understands the manner in which all persons and phenomena exist, i.e. the mind realizing the emptiness of inherent existence.

**Worldly deities and worldly spirits** — beings born in the god realm or as powerful spirits. As they still take rebirth in cyclic existence under the force of disturbing attitudes and karma, their powers are limited and temporary.

**Zen (Ch'an)** — a Mahayana Buddhist tradition popular in China and Japan.

# ADDITIONAL READING

Byles, M. B. *Footprints of Gautama Buddha*. Theosophical Publishing House; Wheaton, 1986.

Dhammananda, K. Sri. *How to Live Without Fear and Worry*. Buddhist Missionary Society; Kuala Lumpur, 1989.

Dhammananda, K. Sri. *What Buddhists Believe*. Buddhist Missionary Society; Kuala Lumpur, 1987.

Dhammananda, K. Sri, ed. *The Dhammapada*. Sasana Abhiwurdhi Wardhana Society; Kuala Lumpur, 1988.

Dharmaraksita. *Wheel of Sharp Weapons*. Library of Tibetan Works and Archives; Dharamsala, India, 1981.

Eppsteiner, Fred, ed. *Path of Compassion*. Parallax; Berkeley, 1988.

Gampopa. *The Jewel Ornament of Liberation*. trans. by Herbert Guenther, Shambhala; Boulder, CO, 1971.

Goldstein, Joseph. *The Experience of Insight*. Shambhala; Boston, 1987.

Gyatso, Geshe Kelsang, *Heart of Wisdom*. Tharpa; London, 1986.

Han, Thich Nhat. *Being Peace*. Parallax; Berkeley.

H.H. Tenzin Gyatso, the 14th Dalai Lama, *Kindness, Clarity and Insight*. Snow Lion; Ithaca, 1984.

H.H. Tenzin Gyatso, the 14th Dalai Lama, *The Dalai Lama at Harvard*. trans. by Jeffrey Hopkins; Snow Lion; Ithaca, 1989.

Kapleau, Philip, ed. *The Three Pillars of Zen*. Rider; London, 1980.

Khema, Ayya. *Being Nobody, Going Nowhere*. Wisdom; Boston, 1987.

Kornfield, Jack and Breiter, Paul, ed. *A Still Forest Pool.* Theosophical Publishing House; Wheaton, Ill., 1987.

Longchenpa, *Kindly Bent to Ease Us.* trans. by Herbert Guenther. Dharma; Emeryville, CA, 1978.

McDonald, Kathleen. *How to Meditate.* Wisdom; Boston, 1984.

Mullin, Glenn. ed. *Essence of Refined Gold.* Snow Lion; Ithaca, 1985.

Mullin, Glenn. trans. *Selected Works of the Dalai Lama VII: Songs of Spiritual Change.* Snow Lion; Ithaca, 1982.

Nyanaponika Thera. *Heart of Buddhist Meditation.* Rider; London, 1962.

Nyanaponika, Thera. *The Power of Mindfulness.* Buddhist Publication Society; Kandy, 1986.

Rabten, Geshe and Dhargye, Geshe. *Advice from a Spiritual Friend,* Wisdom; Boston, 1986.

Rinpoche, Zopa. *Transforming Problems: Utilizing Happiness and Suffering in the Spiritual Path.* Wisdom; Boston, 1987.

Sparham, Gareth, trans. *Tibetan Dhammapada.* Wisdom; Boston, 1983.

Stevenson, Ian. *Cases of the Reincarnation Type.* University of Virginia Press; Charlottesville, 1975. (4 vol.)

Story, Francis. *Rebirth as Doctrine and Experience.* Buddhist Publication Society; Kandy, 1975.

Suzuki, D. T. *An Introduction to Zen Buddhism.* Rider; London, 1969.

Suzuki, Shunriyu. *Zen Mind, Beginner's Mind.* Weatherhill; New York; 1980.